Evolve

INTO A BETTER "US"

Introduction

Relationships require effort and commitment from both partners. Self-accountability plays a crucial role in fostering a healthy and strong connection. In the heat of an argument, focusing on self-accountability may not be the first instinct. Individuals tend to prioritize self-protection by sticking to their own perspectives even if they are in the wrong.

However, practicing individual accountability can enhance and strengthen the bond shared between two people. Beyond personal responsibility, it is essential for both partners must embrace relationship accountability by recognizing how your actions impact your partner and taking ownership of your contributions to any negative patterns in the relationship. Remember, a successful relationship is a collaborative effort.

It's vital to understand blame should not be placed on one person alone when things go wrong in a relationship. Building a thriving partnership requires mutual respect, understanding, and accountability. By acknowledging and working on both individual and relationship accountability, you pave the way for creating a fulfilling relationship and life you both aspire to have.

Plan YOUR GOALS TOGETHER

 GOALS

The SMART goal-setting framework comprises Specific, Measurable, Achievable, Relevant, and Time-bound components. By integrating these aspects into your goal setting, you establish a well-defined path to success. Specific goals offer clarity and direction, measurable goals facilitate progress monitoring, achievable goals set realistic expectations, relevant goals connect with your values and objectives, and time-bound goals create a sense of urgency and accountability. Embracing the SMART methodology transforms your goals from mere aspirations into tangible achievements.

Adopting the SMART approach proves to be a potent strategy in translating your ambitions into realities. Specific goals aid in crystallizing your objectives, while measurable goals provide a means to gauge advancement and maintain motivation. Achievable goals ensure that your targets are feasible, while relevant goals help you stay aligned with your overarching mission. Time-bound goals introduce urgency and accountability, propelling you towards consistent action in pursuit of your aspirations.

Take this opportunity to establish your overarching relationship goals for the upcoming 30 days. Reflect on the manifestations you both aim to achieve within the next five years. Account for each other and think of how you can support one another's dreams. This is the moment to sow the seeds of these aspirations achieving each incremental goals akin to nurtures the growth of your, relationship, dreams, and manifestations. Adhering to the SMART criteria outlined below, commit to weekly reviews together to maintain accountability and remain focused on your objectives.

S	SPECIFIC	WHAT DO WE WANT TO ACCOMPLISH?
M	MEASURABLE	HOW WILL WE KNOW WHEN IT IS ACCOMPLISHED?
A	ACHIEVABLE	HOW CAN THE GOAL BE ACCOMPLISHED?
R	RELEVANT	DOES THIS SEEM WORTHWHILE?
T	TIME BOUND	WHEN CAN WE ACCOMPLISH THIS GOAL?

Communication
SMART TIME-OUT

Now that both of you understand SMART goals, engage in an open discussion about your individual goals and then move on to discussing your goals as a couple. Keep in mind this is not the time for disagreements. Use this chance to identify the aspirations of each partner that contribute to a well-functioning entity called The Relationship. Remember, for the best overall function of a relationship all parties must be present and operating at their best for the overall benefit of the entire unit.

PARTNER 1

_____
_____
_____
_____
_____
_____
_____
_____
_____
_____

PARTNER 2

_____
_____
_____
_____
_____
_____
_____
_____

THE RELATIONSHIP

_____
_____
_____
_____
_____
_____
_____

Accountability IS THE KEY TO SUCCESS

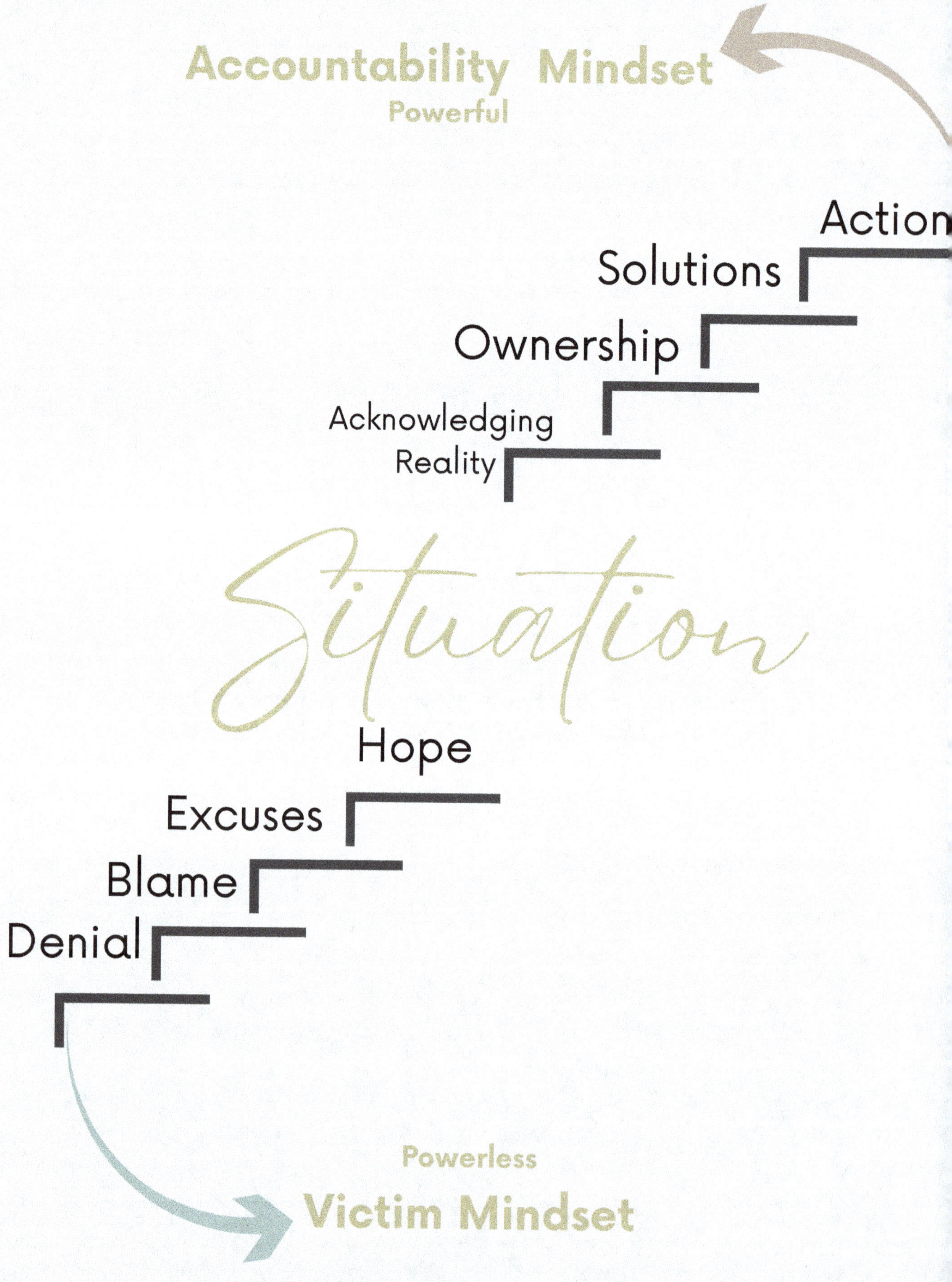

Accountability Mindset
Powerful

Action

Solutions

Ownership

Acknowledging
Reality

Situation

Hope

Excuses

Blame

Denial

Powerless
Victim Mindset

Ladder
OF ACCOUNTABILITY

Denial & Acknowledgment

Denial is the lowest level on the ladder of accountability. When in denial you choose to ignore the issue rather than accept acknowledgement of it. Acknowledgment, on the other hand, marks the first step of taking back power on the ladder. This involves facing the truth head-on, taking responsibility, and making a commitment to change. By embracing acceptance, individuals move beyond denial and towards growth and personal development. Through acceptance true progress and transformation occurs, leading to a more fulfilling and authentic life.

Blame & Ownership

Blame is the second to the lowest on the ladder of accountability. At this level one possesses the idea that others are responsible for the negative situations in life. They participate in excuse making and shifting blame (better known as deflection). Opposite of blame is ownership. With ownership individuals take full responsibility for their actions and their outcomes. When one embraces ownership, they understand they have the power to shape circumstances through their choices and behaviors. Instead of deflecting blame onto others, they actively seek solutions and strive to learn and grow from challenges. By embodying ownership, individuals demonstrate resilience, courage, and a commitment to personal growth and development. Remember, true empowerment comes from owning your story and taking control of your narrative.

Ladder OF ACCOUNTABILITY

Excuses & Solutions

Making excuses only allows one to justify their behavior, choices, or actions. However, true growth and progress come from taking ownership of our mistakes and learning from them. It's important to hold ourselves accountable and use setbacks as opportunities for self-improvement. By taking responsibility for our actions, we empower ourselves to make better decisions in the future and become the best version of ourselves. Instead of making excuses opt for making solutions. Asking "What can I do to fix this?" is a powerful question that shifts our mindset from dwelling on excuses to focusing on solutions. It encourages us to take proactive steps toward resolving issues and moving forward. When we choose to face challenges head-on and seek ways to address them, we demonstrate resilience and determination. Embracing a solution-oriented approach not only helps us overcome obstacles but also strengthens our problem-solving skills and fosters personal growth. Next time you are tempted to make an excuse, challenge yourself to find a solution instead. Your future self will thank you for it.

Hope & Action

Waiting and hoping might not appear negative, but indecision is just as detrimental as making excuses or ignoring the problem. Individuals at this stage acknowledge the issue and its need for action but consciously choose not to act. Those in the action mindset, by contrast, take responsibility for their choices, actions, and decisions, and are dedicated to enhancing the situation.

Self-Accountability
WHAT IS IT?

Self-accountability denotes the capacity to acknowledge repercussions stemming from one's decisions, actions, or conduct. Embracing self-accountability entails acknowledging one's role in each scenario. By taking ownership of the consequences, both favorable and unfavorable, individuals strive to address and rectify the situation to the best of their abilities. Self-accountability, though challenging and daunting, yields significant rewards when striving to cultivate healthy relationships, foster positive social interactions, and build trust and respect.

Understand Your Role

Know your responsibilities
Be clear of commitments

Honesty with Self and Partner
Integrity
Reduces consequences
Don't use to deflect blame
Focus on your own role

Be Quick to Apologize

Recognize you may be wrong
Work to rectify the situation

6
**Behaviors
of Accountability**

Manage Your Time Wisely
Avoid procrastinating
Be aware of time
Show up physically, emotionally, mentally

Your What and Who
Know what You're
Accountable For
and
Who You're
Accountable to

Be Open to Change

Assess the situation
Ask for feedback
Be open to constructive criticism

Relationship Accountability
QUESTIONS

Assuming accountability in a relationship means acknowledging how your actions affect your partner and owning up to your part in any negative patterns hindering the relationship's growth. Keep in mind, both partners must put in effort. It is essential for each individual to be open to self-reflection and take responsibility for their own actions contributing to negative situations in the relationship.

"Did I put in my maximum effort?"
Evaluating individual dedication and effort towards tasks.

"Did I ask if I needed any help?"
Assessing communication skills and being open to seeking help.

Am I completely truthful with myself and my partner?
Encouraging self-awareness and transparency in interactions.

Did I avoid distractions, temptation, and procrastination?
Evaluating the capacity to maintain focus and combat negative influences.

Am I satisfied with my actions?
Reflecting on behavior to ensure alignment with personal values and standards.

How can I do better next time?
Spotting Opportunities for Growth & Gaining Insights from Past Experiences.

HOW TO HOLD YOURSELF ACCOUNTABLE IN THE
Relationship

Regularly ask yourself these questions to create a habit of self-reflection & accountability, contributing to personal growth and a more intentional approach to your actions. This will result in building security, trust , intimacy, and loyalty in your relationship.

Admit Your Mistakes

Acknowledge and take responsibility for your part in the situation.

Take Action to Correct Your Mistake

Take the initiative to address and fix the outcomes of your mistakes.

Don't Make Excuses or Blame Others

Avoid deflection of responsibility and take ownership of your actions.

Maintain honest self-assessment and transparent communication with others.

Be Honest with Yourself and Others

Follow Through on Promises and Commitments

Honor the commitments and promises you make to preserve your integrity and respect.

Embrace the outcomes of your actions, positive or negative, no evasion.

Accept Consequences, Good or Bad

Apologize for Affecting Someone Else

When your actions impact others, take ownership and provide a genuine apology.

Difference

Accountability

Blame

Taking responsibility for honest and ethical behavior towards others.

Obligation or willingness to accept responsibility or to account for one's actions.

Being responsible for decisions made, actions taken, and assignments completed.

Nothing in Common

Blame is the act of censuring, holding responsible, or making negative statements about an individual or group.

To condemn, criticize, denounce, or indict.

Projection- attributing one's shortcomings, mistakes, and misfortunes onto others.

Blaming, also know as projection, is more common in those experiencing negative feelings and are unable to regulate their emotions. Suppressed emotions are those that are hard to regulate and usually emerge as a microaggression initially then graduate to bigger more harmful and hurtful actions.

Hence why it is important to recognize your feelings and actions related to them hold yourself accountable instead of living a life of blame keeping you in a victim mindset.

PARTNER 1 QUESTIONS

Use this accountability chart to self-reflect on any major concerns/issues surrounding the relationship. Be honest with yourself so you can reflect on how you contributed to the situation.

DID I PUT IN MY MAXIMUM EFFORT?	DID I ASK IF I NEEDED ANY HELP?
AM I COMPLETELY TRUTHFUL WITH MYSELF AND THOSE AROUND ME?	DID I AVOID DISTRACTIONS, TEMPTATION, AND PROCRASTINATION?
AM I SATISFIED WITH MY ACTIONS?	HOW CAN I DO BETTER NEXT TIME?

PARTNER 2 QUESTIONS

Use this accountability chart to self-reflect on any major concerns/issues surrounding the relationship. Be honest with yourself so you can reflect on how you contributed to the situation.

DID I PUT IN MY MAXIMUM EFFORT?

DID I ASK IF I NEEDED ANY HELP?

AM I COMPLETELY TRUTHFUL WITH MYSELF AND THOSE AROUND ME?

DID I AVOID DISTRACTIONS, TEMPTATION, AND PROCRASTINATION?

AM I SATISFIED WITH MY ACTIONS?

HOW CAN I DO BETTER NEXT TIME?

Conversations

NAVIGATING DIFFICULT

What are Difficult Conversations?

Difficult conversations arise from topics we struggle to address with someone else, typically stemming from significant differences of opinion and can often envoke strong emotions. These conversations have the potential to evoke emotions.

They can be a deliberate conversation on an uncomfortable subject or a reflection on a negative encounter aiming to exchange viewpoints, foster mutual understanding, and cultivate respect (rather than focusing on persuasion or winning). Even though avoiding such conversations might seem simpler, it could result in escalated conflicts that are more challenging to resolve later.

The Opportunity

Difficult conversations often lead to the most growth and understanding in any relationship. When approached with care and empathy, they provide a pathway to resolution, fostering positive change and strengthening the bond between individuals. By navigating challenging discussions with openness and a willingness to listen, both parties can gain a deeper understanding of each other's perspectives, ultimately building trust and repairing any rifts that may have formed. Embracing difficult conversations as opportunities for growth and connection can pave the way for stronger, more resilient relationships in the long run. Lack of communication and bad communication both lead to the end of a good thing; good communication leads to the end of bad things.

Communication Styles

Passive, Assertive, and Aggressive are the three major communication styles.

PASSIVE	ASSERTIVE	AGGRESSIVE
Avoids and withdraws	Demonstrates wisdom, composure, and attentiveness	Displays rudeness, bossiness, and control; can be disrespectful and create discomfort.
Self-preserves to prevent pain	Shows respect and maturity towards oneself and others	May resort to yelling and screaming.
Confidence deficiency	Avoids overreacting and communicates feelings diplomatically	Projects a sense of superiority over others.
Suppresses emotions	Feels secure, confident, and cherished	Comes across as intimidating.
Prefers safety	Prefers using "I statements" to express thoughts and emotions	
Prioritizes pleasing others over self-acceptance		

Assertive communication involves expressing your feelings clearly, directly, and respectfully. By being assertive, you communicate your thoughts and emotions effectively without being aggressive or disrespectful. Practicing assertive communication aid in reducing conflicts, solving problems efficiently, and empowering yourself.

Check Yourself

- [ ] Make eye contact

- [ ] Be calm and in control

- [ ] Use 'I' statements to express your needs, wants, and feelings

- [ ] Speak confidently without yelling

- [ ] Describe facts without blaming

- [ ] Stand up for yourself

- [ ] Listen to other people without interrupting

- [ ] Be composed

- [ ] Be respectful

- [ ] Say ''No' if you need to

- [ ] Be empathetic to all involved

Using "I" Statements

The key action is to listen with the intent to understand rather than simply respond. If you fail to comprehend the core message, you won't be able to provide an informed reply. Using "I" statements is an effective method for resolving conflicts. When individuals feel accused, it's common to become defensive and emotional; employing the "I" statement structure helps express your emotions and requirements clearly. Taking the time to write these statements down allows for reflection and revision before emotions cloud the true message.

THINK Before you Speak

Relaying negative emotions can hinder communication. Before communicating, ask yourself these questions to ensure you convey in a constructive, not destructive, manner:

IS IT TRUE?

IS IT HELPFUL?

IS IT INSPIRING?

IS IT NECESSARY?

IS IT KIND?

Message
EXAMPLE: USING THE "I" METHOD

By employing this approach, you eliminate the tendency to assign blame. Instead of saying "You did" "He did" or "But, she did" using "I" messages helps communicate your feelings and requirements without shifting blame. Prioritize honesty with yourself first, as betraying yourself is the most severe form of betrayal, then extend that honesty to your partner as not being truthful is equally damaging as self-betrayal.

WHAT ARE MY TRUE FEELINGS?
START WITH "I FEEL/FELT ...."

"I feel hurt"

WHAT WERE THE ACTIONS THAT OFFENDED ME?
START WITH "WHEN .... HAPPENS/HAPPENED"

"When you talk over me"

ULTIMATELY THIS CAUSE ME TO?
START WITH "BECAUSE OF THIS I ...."

"Because of this I shut down"

WHAT I NEED?
START WITH "I NEED .... COMMUNICATION/ACTION TO BETTER UNDERSTAND".

"I need to feel safe sharing my feelings to open up good communication so we can better understand each other"

Construct Your "I" Message

"I feel hurt when you talk over me. Because of this I shut down. I need to feel safe sharing my feelings to open up good communication so we can better understand each other".

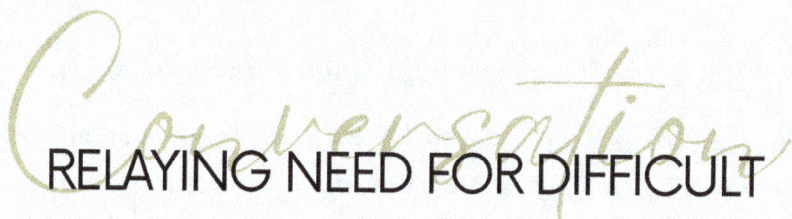

RELAYING NEED FOR DIFFICULT

Understanding how your partner prefers to communicate greatly enhance the way you approach challenging discussions. By adapting to their communication style, you can create a more supportive and productive environment for addressing Difficult Conversations. Whether they prefer a direct approach, a more subtle tone, or a combination of both, being mindful of their preferences can facilitate open and honest communication. Remember, effective communication is a two-way street that requires listening, empathy, and respect. By taking the time to understand and adapt to your partner's communication style, you can navigate Difficult Conversations with greater ease and understanding.

Examples

- Is there a convenient time for us to discuss a matter that could enhance our effectiveness?

- Let's schedule a discussion to address a growing concern. What day is best for you?

- I believe we have differing perspectives on _____. What are your thoughts?

- Our approaches to _____ may vary. Let's try to gain a clearer understanding of _____. I am eager to hear your thoughts and share mine.

Conversation
EXAMPLE: PREPARING FOR THE

Before engaging in a Difficult Conversation, take some time to work through the following worksheet for self-reflection on your thoughts. Schedule a specific time and day to address Difficult Conversations with your partner. If you need to reschedule, that's fine - but don't avoid or delay it. It's crucial not to ambush or bombard your partner. When you are both in a stable emotional and mental state you are open for discussion and resolution of concerns.

The purpose behind the conversation?

"To discuss spending habits"

What do you hope to accomplish?

"Establish budget and emergency fund"

Are your emotions altering your perception?

"Yes, triggered due to growing up poor"

Did you satisfy all the Assertive Communication checks?

"Yes"

Did you complete your Self-Accountability assessment?

"Yes"

What outcome would you like?
"I would like to set up an emergency fund, investing, vacation, and spending budget".

Manifesting

YOUR FUTURE TOGETHER

Manifesting YOUR FUTURE TOGETHER

Manifestation is the practice of thinking aspirational thoughts with the purpose of making them real. I have personally manifested many things; for myself and others. Essentially, you are bringing something into your life through belief. But no manifestations come to fruition without action. In all you do, you must put in work. The essence of an achievement is not created without energy; invoking energy requires actions.

Manifestation is a powerful tool that allows you two to bring your dreams and desires into reality by harnessing the power of positive thinking and belief. It is the art of envisioning your goals as already achieved and taking inspired action toward making them a reality. While manifesting can indeed attract opportunities and blessings into your lives, it is essential to remember it is not a passive process.

To truly manifest the desires of your relationship, you must pair your intentions with consistent effort and action. It is the combination of belief and hard work that propels the relationship's dreams forward and transforms them into tangible results. Every step taken together towards your goals, no matter how small, is a vital piece of the manifestation puzzle.

The universe rewards those who not only dream but also actively pursue their dreams. Embrace the power of manifestation, but never underestimate the importance of dedication, perseverance, and action. With a strong belief in yourself, your relationship, and a commitment to putting in the necessary individual work, you can turn relationship aspirations into achievements and bring the dreams of both partners to life.

THINGS TO REMEMBER WHILE
Manifesting

Express your manifestation in the present tense

Cultivate gratitude and mindfulness every day

Maintain the belief you can achieve your desires

Stay open to receiving

Maintain a positive mindset, particularly at challenging times

Engage in inspired actions daily to bring about concrete outcomes

Monitor your advancements to remain motivated and inspired

Acknowledge and celebrate your successes, regardless of size

Set aside time each day for manifestation and visualization

Embrace the process and remain enjoy the journey!

Manifestations
AVOID SABOTAGING YOUR

Never give up, no matter how challenging the journey may appear!

Refrain from overthinking and worrying about the result

Avoid comparing yourself to others; everyone is on their unique path

Release fear and uncertainty

Trust your intuition and inner guidance

Don't hesitate to seek assistance when necessary

Shift your focus from scarcity to abundance and gratitude

Don't be disheartened if things don't unfold as quickly as anticipated

Keep negative thoughts and conversations at bay

Have a clear vision of what you two want to manifest and to create a roadmap to guide you along the way. Planning helps break down goals into manageable steps, making them more achievable and less overwhelming. By setting specific objectives and deadlines, your relationship vision can remain focused and motivated to work towards your dreams. Remember, successful manifestation is not just about wishing for things to happen - it's about taking action and being intentional about your choices. Follow the action plan below to help you identify and plan your future manifestations.

 ## Identify The Relationship Manifestations

This is the overarching desire. It can be a place, person, thing, or achievement even if your timeline is five or ten years.

 ## Set Deadlines

Make a template that indicating all the tasks and deadlines that you two feel you will need to accomplish to reach the manifestation.

 ## Decide Tools

Determine how you want to manifest this goal or desire. You can be a spiritual as you'd like using candles, dream boards, prayer, meditation, or affirmations.

 ## Establish Follow Up

Ensure you have dedicated follow-up days. This is the time to review your goals and the work you two put into achieving them to determine if you're still in alignment with mastering the manifestation.

 ## Reflection & Adjustment

Reflect to adjust. Reflection allows you two the opportunity to learn and grow giving you valuable insight that will help guide you in adjusting your actions to improve your goals and build on your initial manifestation.

ACTION PLAN

What You Want to Manifest

When setting manifestations, remember to apply the SMART method. Let the manifestations unfold naturally without feeling forced. This approach differs significantly from just setting goals, as you are collaborating with Universal Energy to co-create your life.

Limiting Self Bliefs

These are negative self-perceptions present in our conscious and subconscious mind rooted in past experiences, comments by others, values and beliefs both natured and nurtured. Ask yourself, "What if it weren't true?" and consider what you could achieve if you can walk away from these beliefs.

Affirmations

A message crafted with words to engage both your conscious and unconscious thoughts, inspiring you, challenging you, and propelling you to achieve your utmost potential in life.

We Have, We See, We Are

Visualizations to aid you in painting a mental picture of your desired outcomes. By repeatedly envisioning your goals in vivid detail, you are programming your subconscious mind to work towards turning those visions into reality. This practice helps align your thoughts, emotions, and actions with your intentions, making it easier to attract what you want into your lives. Remember, the more clarity and emotion you infuse into your visualizations, the more powerful they become in shaping your reality. So, keep dreaming big and painting the picture of the life you want to manifest!

ACTION PLAN

Obstacles to Overcome

Life presents both visible and hidden obstacles. Anticipating potential challenges in advance can assist in preparing and strategizing to avoid clear of them. By staying vigilant and proactive, you can navigate through the twists and turns that life may throw your way. Remember, each obstacle is an opportunity for growth and learning. Embrace the challenges, adapt to the changes, and keep moving forward with resilience and determination. With a positive mindset and a strategic approach, you can overcome any hurdle that comes your way. Stay focused, stay determined, and trust in your ability to conquer the obstacles that lie ahead.

Holding Ourselves Accountable

Self-accountability is one of the greatest things a person can possess. Holding yourself accountable allows you to reflect on your choices, learn from your mistakes, and strive to do better in the future. Self-accountability is a key trait of successful individuals who take control of their lives and work towards their goals with determination and resilience. By holding yourself accountable, you embrace personal growth and cultivate a sense of responsibility that guides you towards becoming the best version of yourself. Being the best version of yourself increases the success of your relationship and ensures you bringing your partner the best of you.

I Am Proud of Us

In your manifestation action plan, this section is where you can list your relationship achievements and things you are proud of accomplishing. It's not about fostering arrogance or ego, but rather serves as a reminder of all the amazing things you two have achieved, no matter how big or small.

RELATIONSHIP ACTION PLAN

Time to set your relationship manifestation! This plan will be at the end of each week for you two to reflect and adjust your actions as needed if you deviate from your path.

WE WANT TO MANIFEST	LIMITING BELIEFS	AFFIRMATIONS

WE HAVE	WE SEE	WE ARE

OBSTACLES TO OVERCOME	WAYS TO HOLD OURSELVES ACCOUNTABLE

WE ARE GRATEFUL FOR	WE ARE PROUD OF OURSELVES FOR
○ _____	○ _____
○ _____	○ _____
○ _____	○ _____
○ _____	○ _____

Intimacy

Relationship

Intimacy
RELATIONSHIP

In a relationship, intimacy is the degree of closeness that makes one feel emotionally connected and supported. It involves sharing a wide array of thoughts, emotions, and experiences that are part of the human experience.

Mental Intimacy

Intellectual Intimacy, also known as Mental Intimacy, is a deep connection arising from comprehending each other and sharing innermost thoughts and emotions, enabling partners to understand each other on multiple levels. This form of intimacy is marked by feeling secure in discussing a range of subjects, sharing viewpoints, and remaining receptive to diverse perspectives.

Emotional Intimacy

Emotional Intimacy refers to a deep emotional connection marked by mutual understanding, trust, vulnerability, and communication. Often likened to being perfectly in tune with one another, this bond represents the closeness and trust shared between individuals who feel safe and supported in each other's presence. However, it extends beyond mere closeness, encompassing the concept of another individual truly recognizing, knowing, and understanding you. This level of intimacy involves a profound exploration of each other's inner selves.

Physical Intimacy

Physical intimacy involves closeness and touch between individuals' bodies. This aspect of a romantic relationship can encompass sex, holding hands, cuddling, and kissing. It's important to note physical intimacy is not exclusive to sexual or romantic connections. It fosters trust, warmth, bonding, and closeness amongst all individuals, contributing to emotional well-being and a sense of fulfillment in various relationship dynamics.

Spiritual Intimacy

Spiritual Intimacy commences with one partner disclosing their spiritual beliefs while the other listens in a supportive and non-judgmental manner, fostering spiritual support. By sharing these beliefs, partners strengthen the bond between them, providing the resilience to navigate challenging moments together.

Benefits of Understanding Intimacy

Several studies revealed individuals in long-term committed relationships, such as marriage, often experience better health and longevity. Intimacy plays a crucial role in enhancing connections with others by nurturing trust, empathy, and compassion, which in turn contribute to improved mental, emotional, and spiritual well-being. Prioritizing the highest form of intimacy with your partner can lower stress levels, strengthen unity, diminish feelings of loneliness, enrich sexual connectedness, and alleviate anxiety and depression.

When couples prioritize deep intimate connections and nurture relationship intimacy, they cultivate a strong foundation for their relationship to thrive. Through sharing vulnerabilities, dreams, and fears, they build a bond based on understanding and support. This level of intimacy fosters a sense of security and comfort, allowing individuals to face life's challenges with a united front.

Furthermore, relationships rich in intimacy provide a safe space for personal growth and exploration. Partners empower one another to become the best versions of themselves, encouraging self-improvement and mutual respect. Through intimate communication and shared experiences, couples can create lasting memories and strengthen their emotional connection.

Prioritizing intimacy in a long-term relationship fosters love, understanding, and happiness. By embracing vulnerability, empathy, and compassion, partners build a deep and enduring connection that enriches their lives on multiple levels.

Intimacy ASSESSMENT

Being honest with your self-assessment is important because it helps relay to your partner your intimacy needs and allows you to understand your partner's intimacy needs. Understanding and acknowledging your own vulnerabilities is crucial when it comes to addressing your partner's needs.

Each person in the relationship has their own set of emotional and psychological requirements that must be recognized and respected. It's not just about physical safety; emotional and mental well-being plays a significant role in feeling secure and connected in a partnership.

By neglecting to nurture the various aspects of intimacy in your relationship, you inadvertently leave your partner exposed and vulnerable on a deeper, soulful level. Therefore, it is essential to be mindful and attentive to all facets of intimacy to ensure a strong and protected bond between you and your partner.

Each week you and your partner will complete intimacy assessments in this workbook. These sessions with your partner will involve reassessing if you are meeting each other's intimacy needs. Choose which Partner will be number 1 and number 2. Allow one Partner to write then trade the workbook for the other to write. Set a scheduled time and day for discussion. When you cherish, respect, and genuinely love your partner, their sense of security becomes your own, fostering mutual security and a harmonious fulfilling relationship.

Intimacy
SEMP FOR LOVE

There is no shame in being a SEMP for love. The acronym stands for the four crucial intimacy levels needed to enhance a relationship. Select a specific time and date for both of you to engage in an activity together. Additional lines are available for personalized ideas tailored to your relationship. Write ideas down for your date nights and commit to following through.

Couple Meditation
Grounding Picnic
Couple Fast

_____
_____
_____

♡ Spiritual Intimacy

Enhancing spiritual connection can involve engaging in activities such as prayer, meditation, smudging each other, and fasting together.

Relationship Journal
love Us Jar

_____
_____
_____

♡ Emotional Intimacy

A relationship journal is ideal for couples who lead busy lives, have conflicting schedules, or find it easier to communicate through writing. Another activity for both of you is crafting a "Love Us" jar. Decorate a jar, or box, write love notes, and put them inside the jar. When faced with challenges or during special moments, take out the jar and read the notes together. Return them to the jar once you're done.

Couple Reading
Deck of Love
Hobby Share

_____
_____
_____

♡ Mental Intimacy

Intellectual intimacy involves exchanging ideas, learning together as a couple, and deepening your understanding of your partner. Deck of love requires assigning activities to each suit and numbers being the minutes each activity is carried out. Face cards can represent the length of time you decide. Engaging in active listening exercises, reading together, and involving your partner in your hobbies are all ways to enhance the mental connection in your relationship.

Sip & Soak
Sweet Body Hangman
Reversal Role Play

_____
_____
_____

♡ Physical Intimacy

Activities tro strengthen the physical bond can vary from a 10-minute cuddle session, massages, to trying new experiences. Exploring new activities can help maintain a strong physical connection. Consider a steamy bath or reverse role play. Guess the words your partner writes on your skin (using chocolate, syrup, etc) during a game of sweet hangman.

Evolution
STARTS NOW

YOUR TURN

It's time to put into practice everything you've learned. Take a moment each day to plan: failing to plan is planning to fail. Reflect on your thoughts and feelings at the end of each day. At the end of the week. Review your progress. Remain honest with yourself so you can be true to your relationship.

No peeking at Partner 1's section unless you both have decided to exchange sections before your planned meeting.

Weekly Plan

PARTNER 1

DATE:

M T W T F S S

3 THINGS I AM GRATEFUL FOR:

1. _____
2. _____
3. _____

ISSUES:

SOLUTION:

INTIMACY LEVEL:

ACCOUNTABILITY LEVEL:

5 PRIORITIES:

○
○
○
○
○

THINGS TO GET DONE:

○
○
○
○
○

DATE NIGHT IDEAS:

○
○
○
○
○

MOOD:

RELATIONSHIP GOALS:

1. ○
2. ○
3. ○
4. ○
5. ○

AFFIRMATIONS:

FINANCIAL GOALS:

1.
2.
3.

NOTES:

USE THE NOTES AREA TO ELABORATE ON ISSUES, SELF REFLECTION, AND HOLDING YOURSELF ACCOUNTABLE FOR YOUR CONTRIBUTION TO THE ISSUES. SHARE WITH EACH OTHER DAILY.

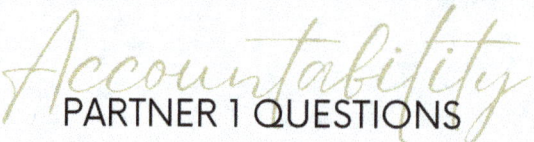

Take this time to work through any issues from the week. Be honest with yourself so you are able to reflect on how you contributed to the situations to prepare for your weekly discussion.

DID I PUT IN MY MAXIMUM EFFORT?

DID I ASK IF I NEEDED ANY HELP?

AM I COMPLETELY TRUTHFUL WITH MYSELF AND THOSE AROUND ME?

DID I AVOID DISTRACTIONS, TEMPTATION, AND PROCRASTINATION?

AM I SATISFIED WITH MY ACTIONS?

HOW CAN I DO BETTER NEXT TIME?

Message

PARTNER 1 "I" METHOD

By employing this approach, you eliminate the tendency to assign blame. Instead of saying "You did", "He did", or "But, she did", using "I" messages helps you communicate your feelings and requirements without shifting blame. Prioritize honesty with yourself first, as betraying yourself is the most severe form of betrayal, then extend that honesty to your partner as not being truthful is equally damaging as self-betrayal.

WHAT ARE MY TRUE FEELINGS? START WITH "I FEEL/FELT …."	**WHAT WERE THE ACTIONS THAT OFFENDED ME?** START WITH "WHEN …. HAPPENS/HAPPENED"
ULTIMATELY THIS CAUSE ME TO? START WITH "BECAUSE OF THIS I …."	**WHAT I NEED?** START WITH "I NEED …. COMMUNICATION/ACTION TO BETTER UNDERSTAND".

Construct Your "I" Message

_____

_____

_____

_____

_____

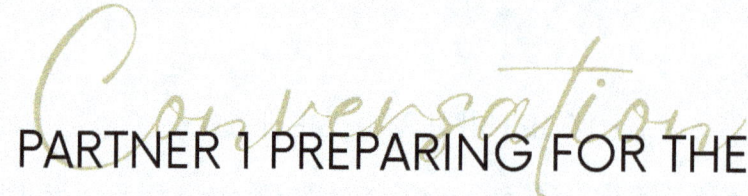

PARTNER 1 PREPARING FOR THE

Before engaging in a Difficult Conversation, take some time to work through the following worksheet for self-reflection on your thoughts. Schedule a specific time and day to address Difficult Conversations with your partner. If you need to reschedule, that's fine - don't avoid or delay it. It's crucial not to ambush or bombard your partner. When you are both in a stable emotional and mental state you are open for discussion and resolution of concerns.

What is the purpose behind the conversation?

What do you hope to accomplish?

Are your emotions altering your perception?

Did you satisfy all the Assertive Communication checks?

Did you complete your Self-Accountability assessment?

What outcome would you like?

PARTNER 1

Remember, lack of communication and bad communication both lead to the ending of a good thing; good communication leads to the end of bad things.

_____

_____

_____

_____

_____

_____

_____

_____

_____

_____

_____

_____

_____

_____

_____

_____

_____

Intimacy
PARTNER 1 NEEDS

Identify the level of the intimacy you currently receive from your partner by shading up to the wave level. It's crucial to be open and sincere. Your partner won't be able to adapt to your needs unless they understand what's missing.

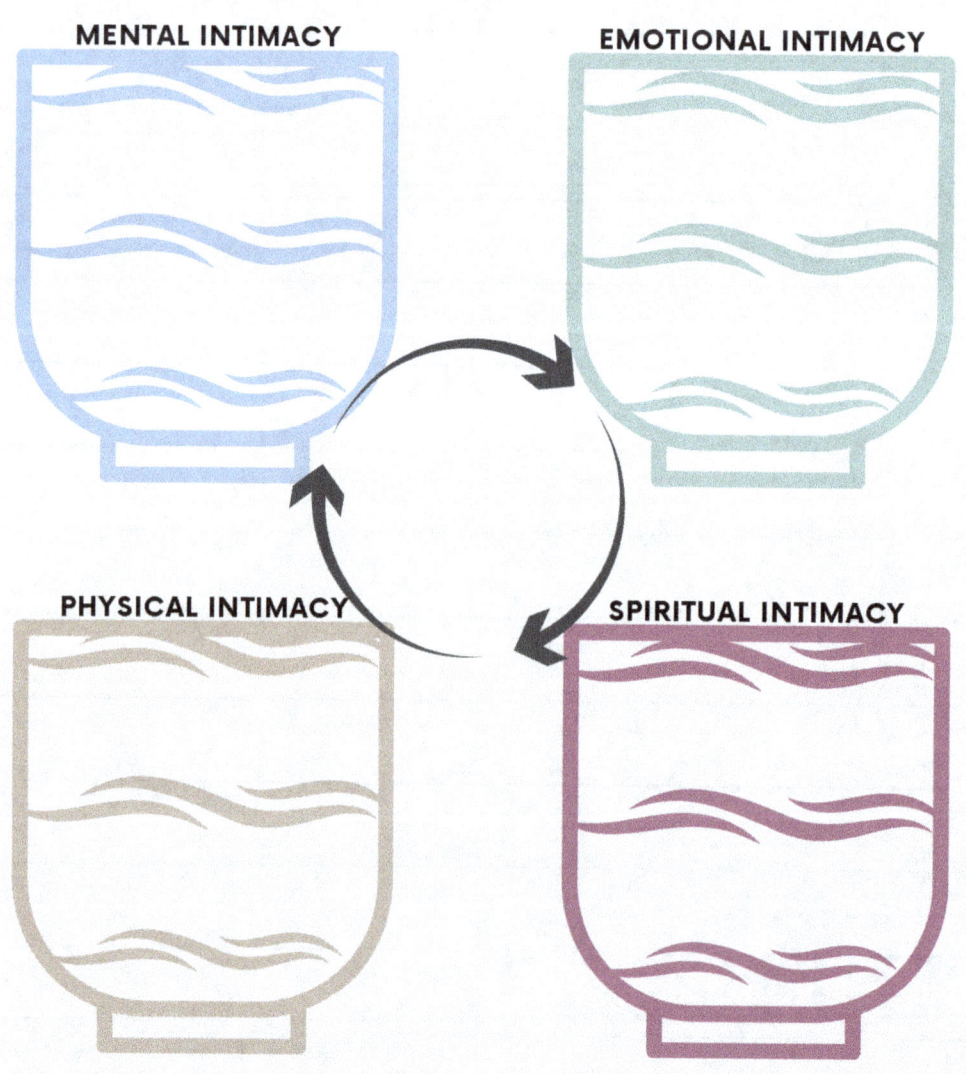

MENTAL INTIMACY

EMOTIONAL INTIMACY

PHYSICAL INTIMACY

SPIRITUAL INTIMACY

Partner 2

YOUR TURN

No peeking at Partner 1's section unless you both have decided to exchange sections before your planned meeting.

Weekly Plan

PARTNER 2

DATE:

M T W T F S S

3 THINGS I AM GRATEFUL FOR:

1. _____
2. _____
3. _____

ISSUES:

SOLUTION:

INTIMACY LEVEL:

ACCOUNTABILITY LEVEL:

5 PRIORITIES:
- ○ _____
- ○ _____
- ○ _____
- ○ _____
- ○ _____

THINGS TO GET DONE:
- ○ _____
- ○ _____
- ○ _____
- ○ _____
- ○ _____

DATE NIGHT IDEAS:
- ○ _____
- ○ _____
- ○ _____
- ○ _____

MOOD:

RELATIONSHIP GOALS:

1. ○
2. ○
3. ○
4. ○
5. ○

AFFIRMATIONS:

FINANCIAL GOALS:

1. _____
2. _____
3. _____

NOTES:

USE THE NOTES AREA TO ELABORATE ON ISSUES, SELF REFLECTION, AND HOLDING YOURSELF ACCOUNTABLE FOR YOUR CONTRIBUTION TO THE ISSUES. SHARE WITH EACH OTHER DAILY.

Take this time to work through any issues from the week. Be honest with yourself so you can reflect on how you contributed to the situations to prepare for your weekly discussion.

DID I PUT IN MY MAXIMUM EFFORT?

DID I ASK IF I NEEDED ANY HELP?

AM I COMPLETELY TRUTHFUL WITH MYSELF AND THOSE AROUND ME?

DID I AVOID DISTRACTIONS, TEMPTATION, AND PROCRASTINATION?

AM I SATISFIED WITH MY ACTIONS?

HOW CAN I DO BETTER NEXT TIME?

Message

By employing this approach, you eliminate the tendency to assign blame. Instead of saying "You did", "He did", or "But, she did", using "I" messages helps you communicate your feelings and requirements without shifting blame. Prioritize honesty with yourself first, as betraying yourself is the most severe form of betrayal, then extend that honesty to your partner as not being truthful is equally damaging as self-betrayal.

WHAT ARE MY TRUE FEELINGS?
START WITH "I FEEL/FELT ...."

WHAT WERE THE ACTIONS THAT OFFENDED ME?
START WITH "WHEN .... HAPPENS/HAPPENED"

ULTIMATELY THIS CAUSE ME TO?
START WITH "BECAUSE OF THIS I ...."

WHAT I NEED?
START WITH "I NEED ....
COMMUNICATION/ACTION TO BETTER UNDERSTAND".

Construct Your "I" Message

_____

_____

_____

_____

46

PARTNER 2 PREPARING FOR THE *Conversation*

Before engaging in a Difficult Conversation, take some time to work through the following worksheet for self-reflection on your thoughts. Schedule a specific time and day to address Difficult Conversations with your partner. If you need to reschedule, that's fine - but don't avoid or delay it. It's crucial not to ambush or bombard your partner. When you are both in a stable emotional and mental state you are open for discussion and resolution of concerns.

What is the purpose behind the conversation?

What do you hope to accomplish?

Are your emotions altering your perception?

Did you satisfy all the Assertive Communication checks?

Did you complete your Self-Accountability assessment?

What outcome would you like?

Communication

PARTNER 2

Remember, lack of communication and bad communication both lead to the ending of a good thing; good communication leads to the end of bad things.

Intimacy
PARTNER 2 NEEDS

Identify the level of the intimacy you currently receive from your partner by shading up to the wave level. It's crucial to be open and sincere. Your partner won't be able to adapt to your needs unless they understand what's missing.

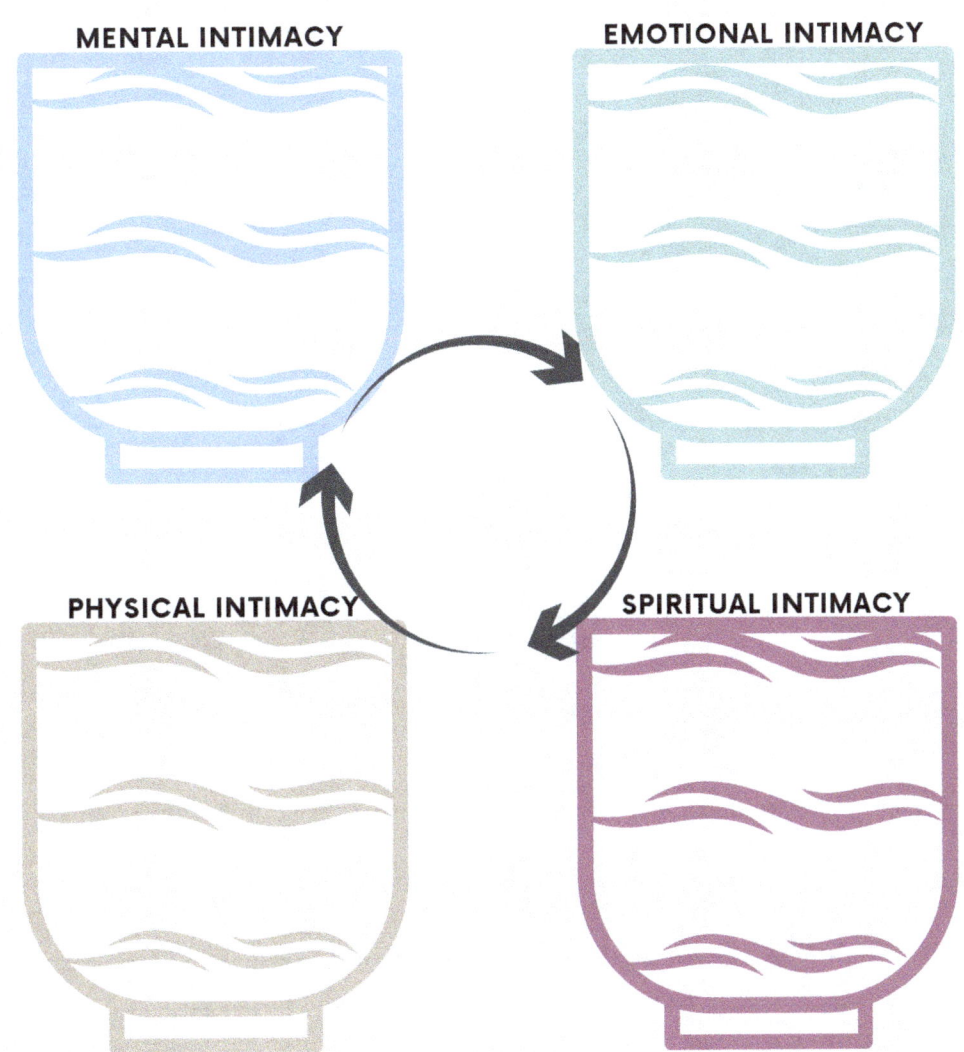

MENTAL INTIMACY

EMOTIONAL INTIMACY

PHYSICAL INTIMACY

SPIRITUAL INTIMACY

COMMUNICATING TOGETHER

Congratulations on successfully completing a challenging journey. Throughout this experience, you have mastered the SMART method for setting goals collaboratively. You've delved into self and relationship accountability, pushing beyond your comfort zones. Together, you have enhanced trust by learning how to articulate thoughts and communicate effectively during tough discussions. Additionally, you've recognized various forms of relationship intimacy. Utilize these tools to engage in open communication and how it affects 'The Relationship'. Work together to understand the impact of specific topics on your relationship and plan a path forward.

PARTNER 1

_____
_____
_____
_____
_____
_____
_____
_____
_____
_____

PARTNER 2

_____
_____
_____
_____
_____
_____
_____
_____
_____
_____

THE RELATIONSHIP

_____
_____
_____
_____
_____
_____
_____
_____

Intimacy
RELATIONSHIP NEEDS

Identify the level of intimacy you and your partner feel The Relationship is currently receives from both of you by shading up to the waves. It's crucial to be open and sincere. Imagine your relationship as a living entity, constantly evolving and growing. By acknowledging the level of intimacy you and your partner are providing, you can nurture and strengthen this bond. Remember, the relationship exists independently of each of you, with its own set of needs. By coming together and understanding these dynamics, you can navigate the levels of intimacy with grace and compassion.

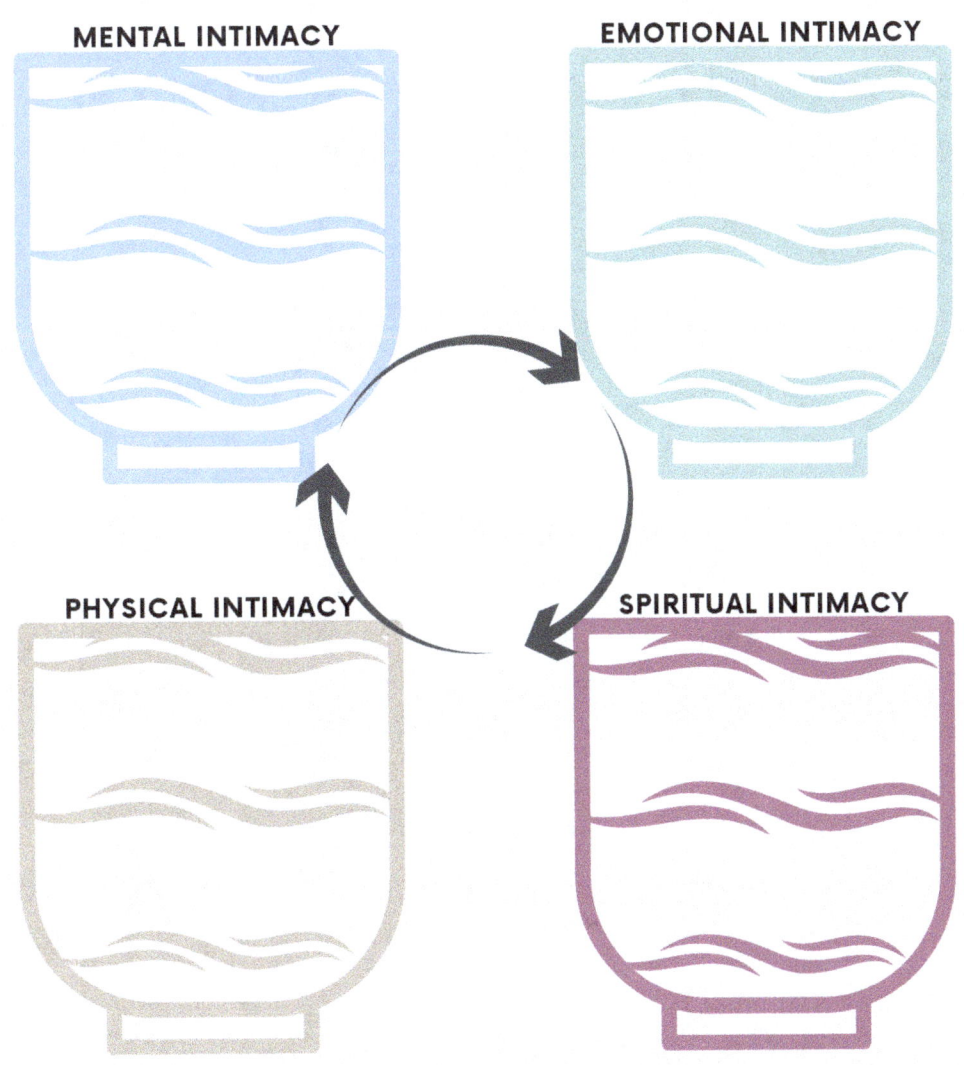

MENTAL INTIMACY

EMOTIONAL INTIMACY

PHYSICAL INTIMACY

SPIRITUAL INTIMACY

Week TWO

YOUR TURN

Allow this journey to be the greatest gift you can give yourself. By nurturing your relationship's growth and well-being, you sow the seeds for a more fulfilling and enriched life. Embrace this journey with open arms and a curious mind, for within The Relationship lies endless potential waiting to be unlocked. Cherish the gift of companionship and watch as it transforms you into the best version of yourself.

No peeking at Partner 2's section unless you both have decided to exchange sections before your planned meeting.

Weekly Plan

PARTNER 1

DATE:

M T W T F S S

3 THINGS I AM GRATEFUL FOR:

1. _____
2. _____
3. _____

ISSUES:

SOLUTION:

INTIMACY LEVEL:

ACCOUNTABILITY LEVEL:

5 PRIORITIES:
- ◯
- ◯
- ◯
- ◯
- ◯

THINGS TO GET DONE:
- ◯
- ◯
- ◯
- ◯
- ◯

DATE NIGHT IDEAS:
- ◯
- ◯
- ◯
- ◯
- ◯

MOOD:

RELATIONSHIP GOALS:
1. ◯
2. ◯
3. ◯
4. ◯
5. ◯

AFFIRMATIONS:

FINANCIAL GOALS:
1.
2.
3.

NOTES:

USE THE NOTES AREA TO ELABORATE ON ISSUES, SELF REFLECTION, AND HOLDING YOURSELF ACCOUNTABLE FOR YOUR CONTRIBUTION TO THE ISSUES. SHARE WITH EACH OTHER DAILY.

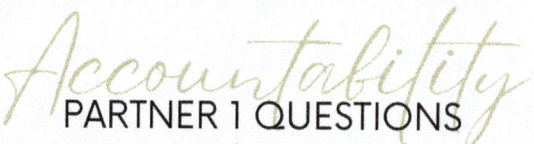

Take this time to work through any issues from the week. Be honest with yourself so you can reflect on how you contributed to the situations to prepare for your weekly discussion.

DID I PUT IN MY MAXIMUM EFFORT?

DID I ASK IF I NEEDED ANY HELP?

AM I COMPLETELY TRUTHFUL WITH MYSELF AND THOSE AROUND ME?

DID I AVOID DISTRACTIONS, TEMPTATION, AND PROCRASTINATION?

AM I SATISFIED WITH MY ACTIONS?

HOW CAN I DO BETTER NEXT TIME?

Message

PARTNER 1 "I" METHOD

By employing this approach, you eliminate the tendency to assign blame. Instead of saying "You did", "He did", or "But, she did", using "I" messages helps you communicate your feelings and requirements without shifting blame. Prioritize honesty with yourself first, as betraying yourself is the most severe form of betrayal, then extend that honesty to your partner as not being truthful is equally damaging as self-betrayal.

WHAT ARE MY TRUE FEELINGS?
START WITH "I FEEL/FELT ...."

WHAT WERE THE ACTIONS THAT OFFENDED ME?
START WITH "WHEN .... HAPPENS/HAPPENED"

ULTIMATELY THIS CAUSE ME TO?
START WITH "BECAUSE OF THIS I ...."

WHAT I NEED?
START WITH "I NEED ....
COMMUNICATION/ACTION TO BETTER UNDERSTAND".

Construct Your "I" Message

_____

_____

_____

_____

_____

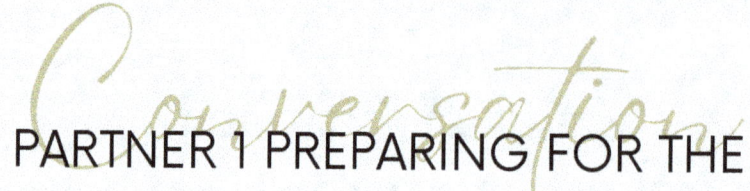

PARTNER 1 PREPARING FOR THE

Before engaging in a Difficult Conversation, take some time to work through the following worksheet for self-reflection on your thoughts. Schedule a specific time and day to address Difficult Conversations with your partner. If you need to reschedule, that's fine - but don't avoid or delay it. It's crucial not to ambush or bombard your partner. When you are both in a stable emotional and mental state you are open for discussion and resolution of concerns.

What is the purpose behind the conversation?

What do you hope to accomplish?

Are your emotions altering your perception?

Did you satisfy all the Assertive Communication checks?

Did you complete your Self-Accountability assessment?

What outcome would you like?

PARTNER 1

Remember, lack of communication and bad communication both lead to the ending of a good thing; good communication leads to the end of bad things.

_____

_____

_____

_____

_____

_____

_____

_____

_____

_____

_____

_____

_____

_____

_____

_____

_____

Intimacy
PARTNER 1 NEEDS

Identify the level of the intimacy you currently receive from your partner by shading up to the wave level. It's crucial to be open and sincere. Your partner won't be able to adapt to your needs unless they understand what's missing.

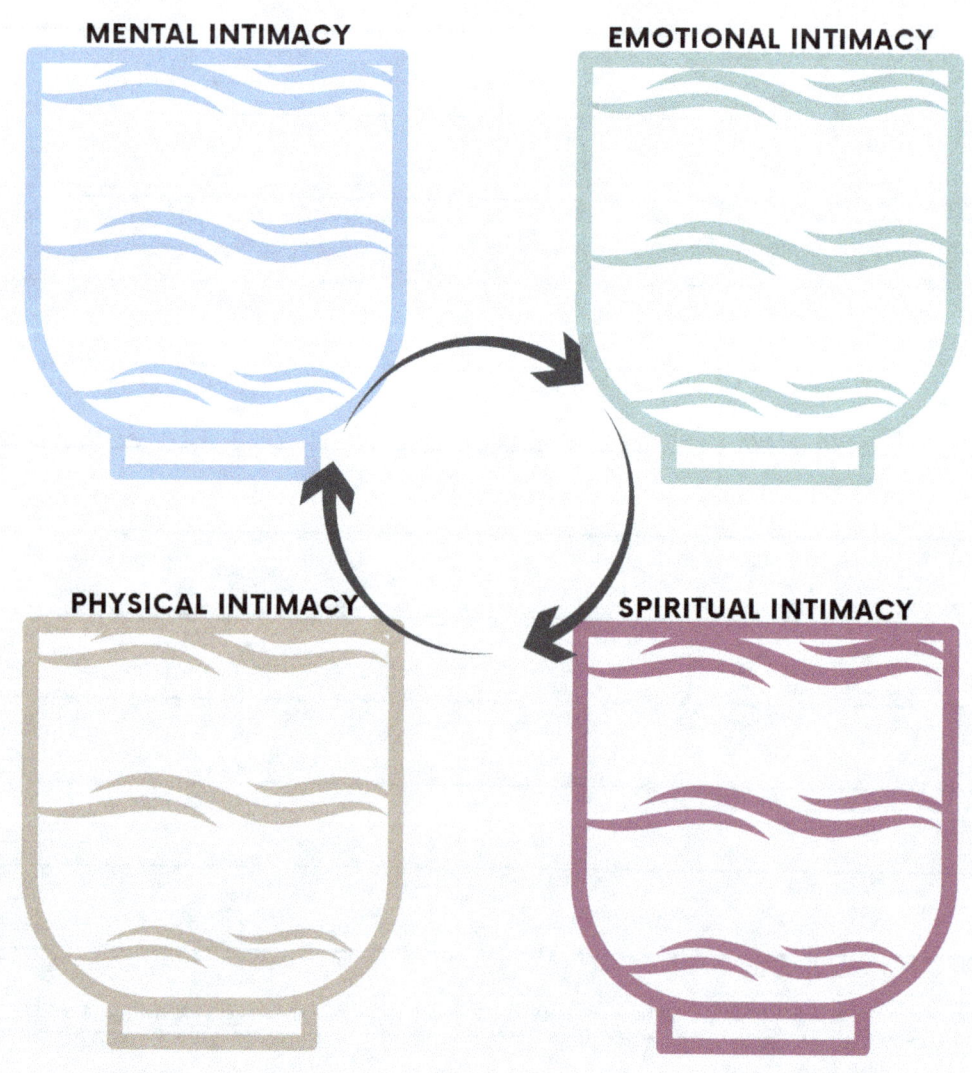

MENTAL INTIMACY

EMOTIONAL INTIMACY

PHYSICAL INTIMACY

SPIRITUAL INTIMACY

Partner 2

YOUR TURN

No peeking at Partner 1's section unless you both have decided to exchange sections before your planned meeting.

Weekly Plan

PARTNER 2

DATE:

M T W T F S S

3 THINGS I AM GRATEFUL FOR:

1.
2.
3.

ISSUES:

SOLUTION:

INTIMACY LEVEL:

ACCOUNTABILITY LEVEL:

5 PRIORITIES:

○
○
○
○
○

THINGS TO GET DONE:

○
○
○
○
○

DATE NIGHT IDEAS:

○
○
○
○

MOOD:

RELATIONSHIP GOALS:

1. ○
2. ○
3. ○
4. ○
5. ○

AFFIRMATIONS:

FINANCIAL GOALS:

1.
2.
3.

NOTES:

USE THE NOTES AREA TO ELABORATE ON ISSUES, SELF REFLECTION, AND HOLDING YOURSELF ACCOUNTABLE FOR YOUR CONTRIBUTION TO THE ISSUES. SHARE WITH EACH OTHER DAILY.

Accountability
PARTNER 2 QUESTIONS

Take this time to work through any issues from the week. Be honest with yourself so you can reflect on how you contributed to the situations to prepare for your weekly discussion.

DID I PUT IN MY MAXIMUM EFFORT?

DID I ASK IF I NEEDED ANY HELP?

AM I COMPLETELY TRUTHFUL WITH MYSELF AND THOSE AROUND ME?

DID I AVOID DISTRACTIONS, TEMPTATION, AND PROCRASTINATION?

AM I SATISFIED WITH MY ACTIONS?

HOW CAN I DO BETTER NEXT TIME?

Message

By employing this approach, you eliminate the tendency to assign blame. Instead of saying "You did", "He did", or "But, she did", using "I" messages helps you communicate your feelings and requirements without shifting blame. Prioritize honesty with yourself first, as betraying yourself is the most severe form of betrayal, then extend that honesty to your partner as not being truthful is equally damaging as self-betrayal.

WHAT ARE MY TRUE FEELINGS?
START WITH "I FEEL/FELT ...."

WHAT WERE THE ACTIONS THAT OFFENDED ME?
START WITH "WHEN .... HAPPENS/HAPPENED"

ULTIMATELY THIS CAUSE ME TO?
START WITH "BECAUSE OF THIS I ...."

WHAT I NEED?
START WITH "I NEED ....
COMMUNICATION/ACTION TO BETTER UNDERSTAND".

Construct Your "I" Message

_____

_____

_____

_____

_____

PARTNER 2 PREPARING FOR THE *Conversation*

Before engaging in a Difficult Conversation, take some time to work through the following worksheet for self-reflection on your thoughts. Schedule a specific time and day to address Difficult Conversations with your partner. If you need to reschedule, that's fine - but don't avoid or delay it. It's crucial not to ambush or bombard your partner. When you are both in a stable emotional and mental state, you are open for discussion and resolution of concerns.

What is the purpose behind the conversation?

What do you hope to accomplish?

Are your emotions altering your perception?

Did you satisfy all the Assertive Communication checks?

Did you complete your Self-Accountability assessment?

What outcome would you like?

Communication
PARTNER 2

Remember, lack of communication and bad communication both lead to the ending of a good thing; good communication leads to the end of bad things.

_____

_____

_____

_____

_____

_____

_____

_____

_____

_____

_____

_____

_____

_____

_____

Intimacy
PARTNER 2 NEEDS

Identify the level of the intimacy you currently receive from your partner by shading up to the wave level. It's crucial to be open and sincere. Your partner won't be able to adapt to your needs unless they understand what's missing.

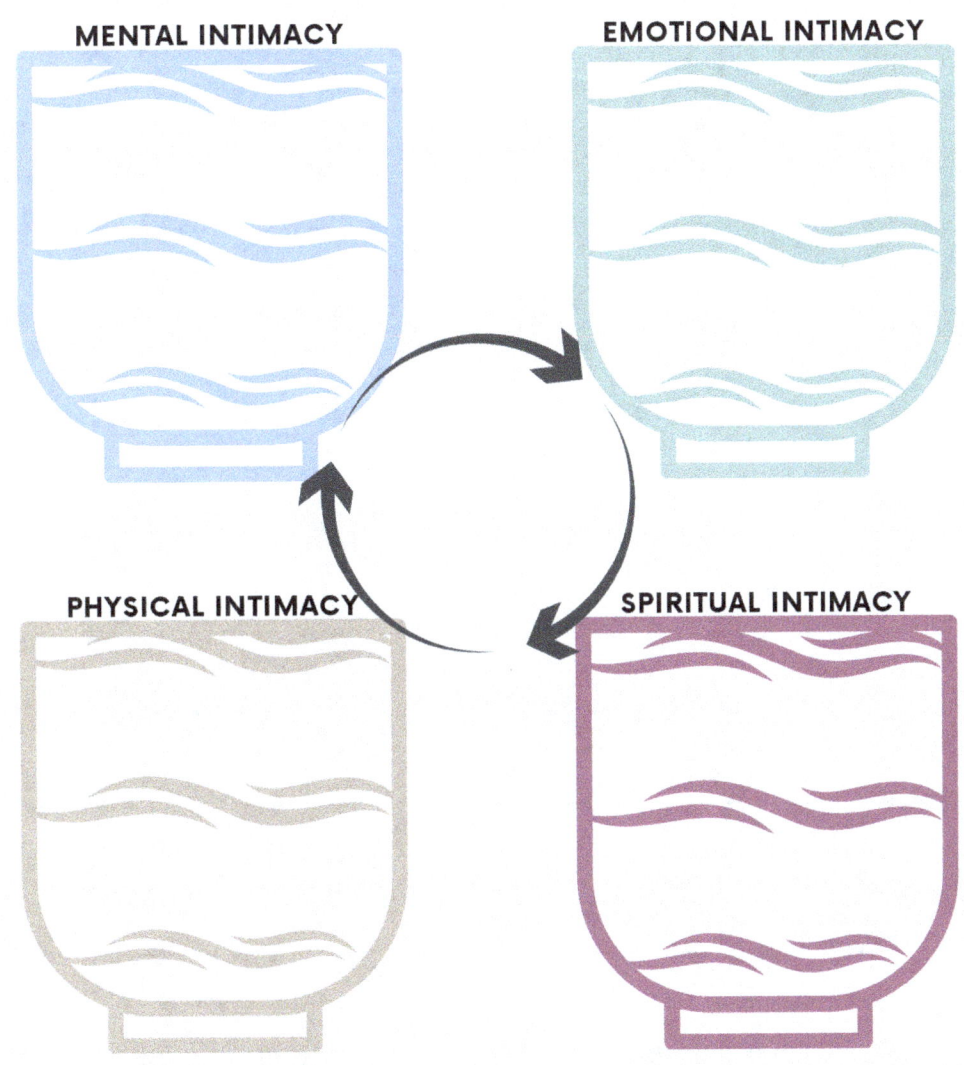

MENTAL INTIMACY

EMOTIONAL INTIMACY

PHYSICAL INTIMACY

SPIRITUAL INTIMACY

COMMUNICATING TOGETHER

Congratulations on successfully completing a challenging journey. Throughout this experience, you have mastered the SMART method for setting goals collaboratively. You've delved into self and relationship accountability, pushing beyond your comfort zones. Together, you have enhanced trust by learning how to articulate thoughts and communicate effectively during tough discussions. Additionally, you've recognized various forms of relationship intimacy. Utilize these tools to engage in open communication and how it affects 'The Relationship'. Work together to understand the impact of specific topics on your relationship and plan a path forward.

PARTNER 1

_____
_____
_____
_____
_____
_____
_____
_____
_____
_____

PARTNER 2

_____
_____
_____
_____
_____
_____
_____
_____
_____
_____

THE RELATIONSHIP

_____
_____
_____
_____
_____
_____
_____
_____

Intimacy
RELATIONSHIP NEEDS

Identify the level of the intimacy you and your partner feel The Relationship currently receives from both of you by shading up to the wave level. It's crucial to be open and sincere. Imagine your relationship as a living entity, constantly evolving and growing. By acknowledging the level of intimacy you and your partner are providing, you can nurture and strengthen this bond. Remember, the relationship exists independently of each of you, with its own set of needs. By coming together and understanding these dynamics, you can navigate the levels of intimacy with grace and compassion.

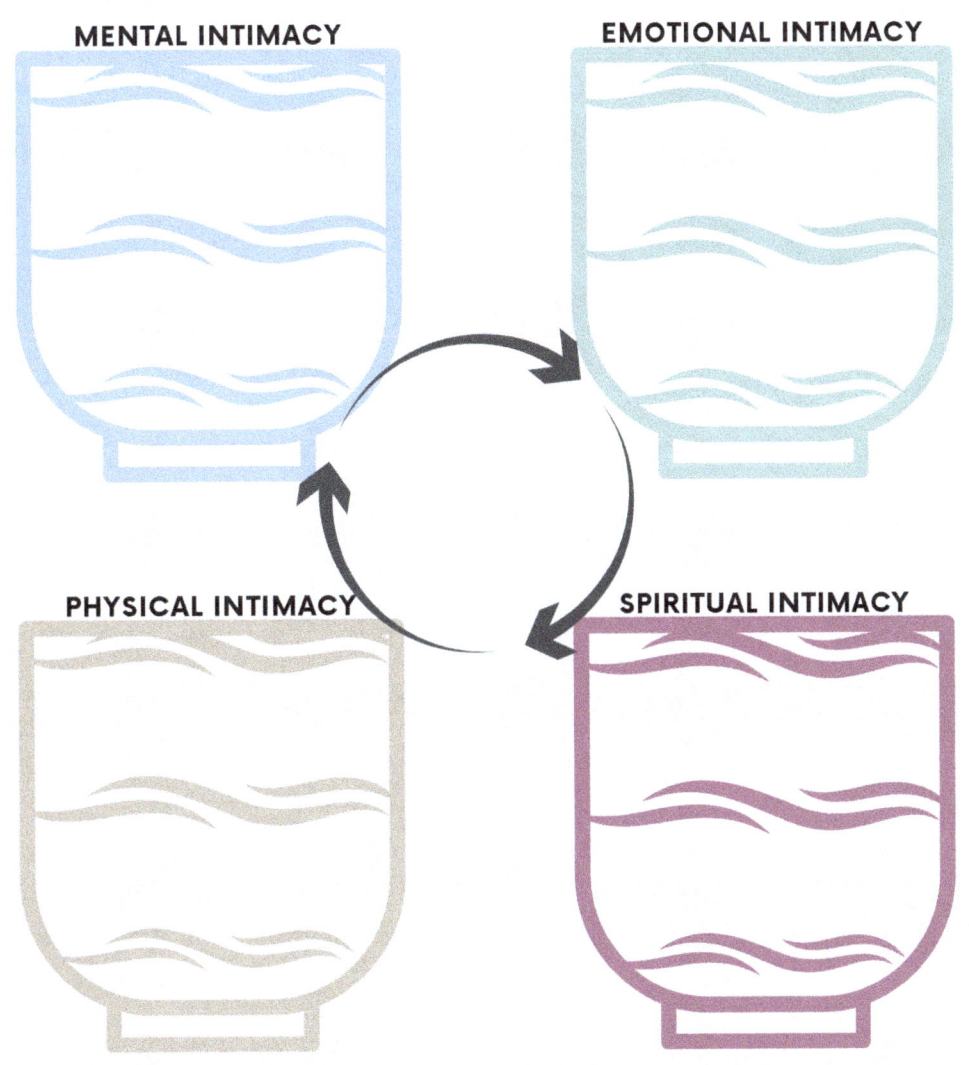

MENTAL INTIMACY

EMOTIONAL INTIMACY

PHYSICAL INTIMACY

SPIRITUAL INTIMACY

Week

THREE

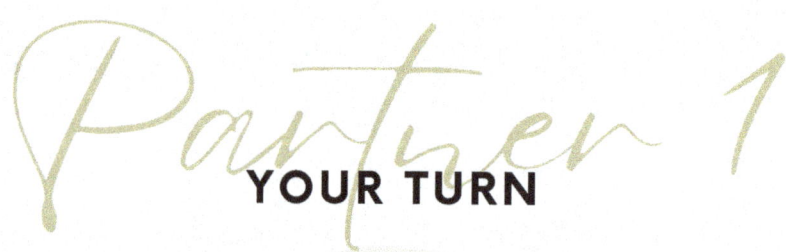

Taking ownership of your actions and decisions is a fundamental aspect of personal growth and development. By holding yourself accountable, you demonstrate the level of maturity and responsibility required to maintain a healthy and successful relationship. When you accept responsibility for your mistakes and actively work towards improvement, you not only build integrity within yourself but also earn the respect and trust of your Partner.

No peeking at Partner 2's section unless you both have decided to exchange sections before your planned meeting.

Weekly Plan

PARTNER 1

DATE:

M T W T F S S

3 THINGS I AM GRATEFUL FOR:

1. _____
2. _____
3. _____

ISSUES:

SOLUTION:

INTIMACY LEVEL:

ACCOUNTABILITY LEVEL:

5 PRIORITIES:
○ _____
○ _____
○ _____
○ _____
○ _____

THINGS TO GET DONE:
○ _____
○ _____
○ _____
○ _____
○ _____

DATE NIGHT IDEAS:
○ _____
○ _____
○ _____
○ _____
○ _____

MOOD:

RELATIONSHIP GOALS:
1. _____ ○
2. _____ ○
3. _____ ○
4. _____ ○
5. _____ ○

AFFIRMATIONS:

FINANCIAL GOALS:
1. _____
2. _____
3. _____

NOTES:

USE THE NOTES AREA TO ELABORATE ON ISSUES, SELF REFLECTION, AND HOLDING YOURSELF ACCOUNTABLE FOR YOUR CONTRIBUTION TO THE ISSUES. SHARE WITH EACH OTHER DAILY.

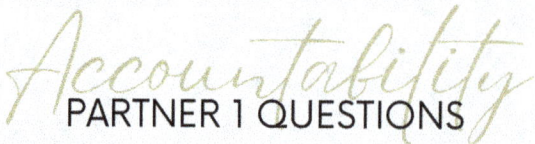

Take this time to work through any issues from the week. Be honest with yourself so you can reflect on how you contributed to the situations to prepare for your weekly discussion.

DID I PUT IN MY MAXIMUM EFFORT?

DID I ASK IF I NEEDED ANY HELP?

AM I COMPLETELY TRUTHFUL WITH MYSELF AND THOSE AROUND ME?

DID I AVOID DISTRACTIONS, TEMPTATION, AND PROCRASTINATION?

AM I SATISFIED WITH MY ACTIONS?

HOW CAN I DO BETTER NEXT TIME?

PARTNER 1 "I" METHOD

By employing this approach, you eliminate the tendency to assign blame. Instead of saying "You did", "He did", or "But, she did", using "I" messages helps you communicate your feelings and requirements without shifting blame. Prioritize honesty with yourself first, as betraying yourself is the most severe form of betrayal, then extend that honesty to your partner as not being truthful is equally damaging as self-betrayal.

WHAT ARE MY TRUE FEELINGS?
START WITH "I FEEL/FELT ...."

WHAT WERE THE ACTIONS THAT OFFENDED ME?
START WITH "WHEN .... HAPPENS/HAPPENED"

ULTIMATELY THIS CAUSE ME TO?
START WITH "BECAUSE OF THIS I ...."

WHAT I NEED?
START WITH "I NEED .... COMMUNICATION/ACTION TO BETTER UNDERSTAND".

Construct Your "I" Message

_____

_____

_____

_____

_____

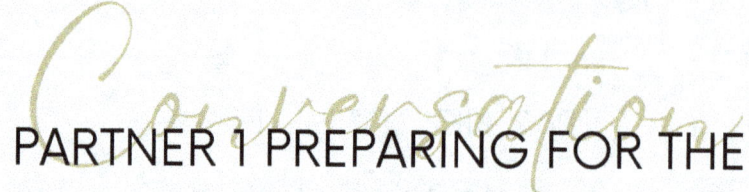

PARTNER 1 PREPARING FOR THE

Before engaging in a Difficult Conversation, take some time to work through the following worksheet for self-reflection on your thoughts. Schedule a specific time and day to address Difficult Conversations with your partner. If you need to reschedule, that's fine - but don't avoid or delay it. It's crucial not to ambush or bombard your partner. When you are both in a stable emotional and mental state, you are open for discussion and resolution of concerns.

what is the purpose behind the conversation?

What do you hope to accomplish?

Are your emotions altering your perception?

Did you satisfy all the Assertive Communication checks?

Did you complete your Self-Accountability assessment?

What outcome would you like?

Communication

PARTNER 1

Remember, lack of communication and bad communication both lead to the ending of a good thing; good communication leads to the end of bad things.

_____

_____

_____

_____

_____

_____

_____

_____

_____

_____

_____

_____

_____

_____

_____

_____

Intimacy
PARTNER 1 NEEDS

Identify the level of the intimacy youu currently receive from your partner by shading up to the wave level. It's crucial to be open and sincere. Your partner won't be able to adapt to your needs unless they understand what's missing.

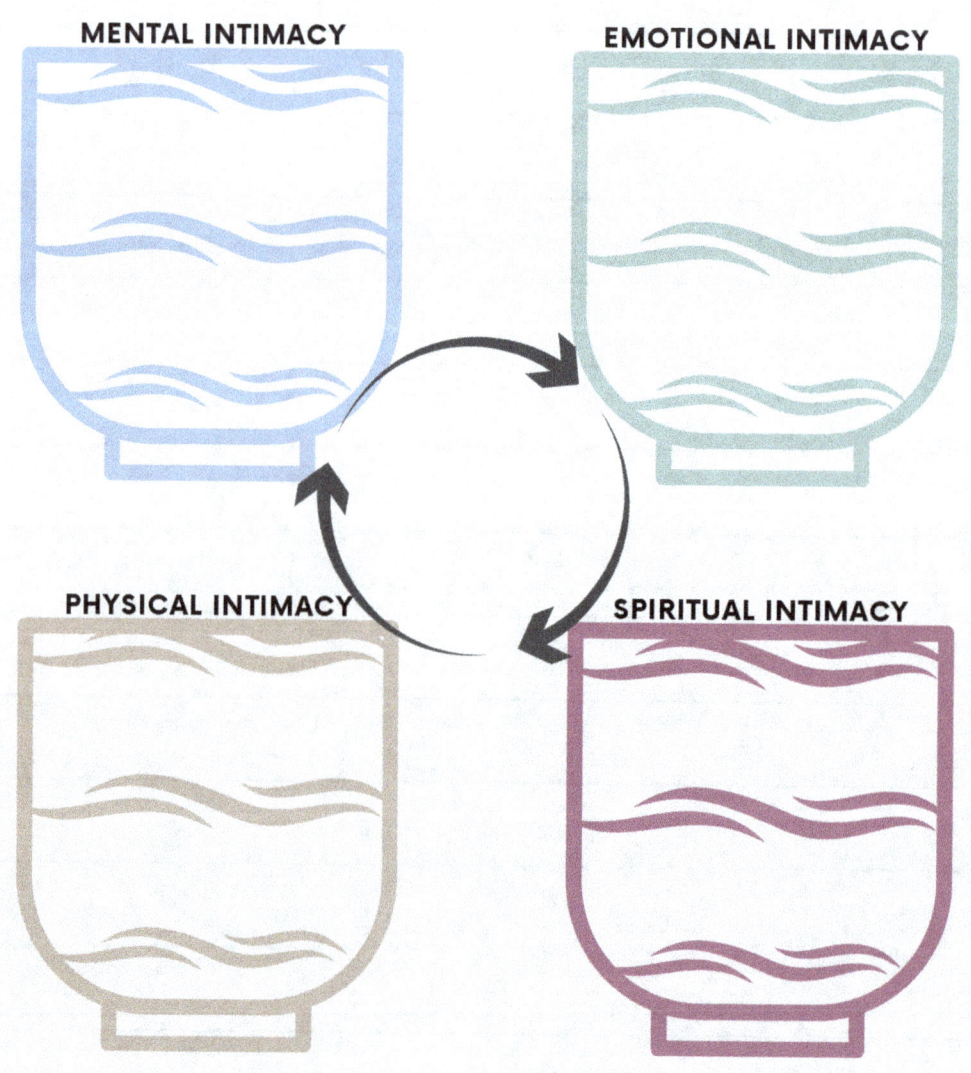

MENTAL INTIMACY

EMOTIONAL INTIMACY

PHYSICAL INTIMACY

SPIRITUAL INTIMACY

Partner 2

YOUR TURN

No peeking at Partner 1's section unless you both have decided to exchange sections before your planned meeting.

Weekly Plan

PARTNER 2

DATE:

M	T	W	T	F	S	S

3 THINGS I AM GRATEFUL FOR:

1. _____
2. _____
3. _____

ISSUES:

SOLUTION:

INTIMACY LEVEL:

ACCOUNTABILITY LEVEL:

5 PRIORITIES:

- ○ _____
- ○ _____
- ○ _____
- ○ _____
- ○ _____

THINGS TO GET DONE:

- ○ _____
- ○ _____
- ○ _____
- ○ _____
- ○ _____

DATE NIGHT IDEAS:

- ○ _____
- ○ _____
- ○ _____
- ○ _____

MOOD:

RELATIONSHIP GOALS:

1. ○
2. ○
3. ○
4. ○
5. ○

AFFIRMATIONS:

FINANCIAL GOALS:

1. _____
2. _____
3. _____

NOTES:

USE THE NOTES AREA TO ELABORATE ON ISSUES, SELF REFLECTION, AND HOLDING YOURSELF ACCOUNTABLE FOR YOUR CONTRIBUTION TO THE ISSUES. SHARE WITH EACH OTHER DAILY.

PARTNER 2 QUESTIONS

Take this time to work through any issues from the week. Be honest with yourself so can reflect on how you contributed to the situations to prepare for your weekly discussion.

DID I PUT IN MY MAXIMUM EFFORT?

DID I ASK IF I NEEDED ANY HELP?

AM I COMPLETELY TRUTHFUL WITH MYSELF AND THOSE AROUND ME?

DID I AVOID DISTRACTIONS, TEMPTATION, AND PROCRASTINATION?

AM I SATISFIED WITH MY ACTIONS?

HOW CAN I DO BETTER NEXT TIME?

Message

By employing this approach, you eliminate the tendency to assign blame. Instead of saying "You did", "He did", or "But, she did", using "I" messages helps you communicate your feelings and requirements without shifting blame. Prioritize honesty with yourself first, as betraying yourself is the most severe form of betrayal, then extend that honesty to your partner as not being truthful is equally damaging as self-betrayal.

WHAT ARE MY TRUE FEELINGS?
START WITH "I FEEL/FELT ...."

WHAT WERE THE ACTIONS THAT OFFENDED ME?
START WITH "WHEN .... HAPPENS/HAPPENED"

ULTIMATELY THIS CAUSE ME TO?
START WITH "BECAUSE OF THIS I ...."

WHAT I NEED?
START WITH "I NEED .... COMMUNICATION/ACTION TO BETTER UNDERSTAND".

Construct Your "I" Message

_____

_____

_____

_____

_____

PARTNER 2 PREPARING FOR THE
Conversation

Before engaging in a Difficult Conversation, take some time to work through the following worksheet for self-reflection on your thoughts. Schedule a specific time and day to address Difficult Conversations with your partner. If you need to reschedule, that's fine - but don't avoid or delay it. It's crucial not to ambush or bombard your partner. When you are both in a stable emotional and mental state, you are open for discussion and resolution of concerns.

What is the purpose behind the conversation?

What do you hope to accomplish?

Are your emotions altering your perception?

Did you satisfy all the Assertive Communication checks?

Did you complete your Self-Accountability assessment?

What outcome would you like?

PARTNER 2

Remember, lack of communication and bad communication both lead to the ending of a good thing; good communication leads to the end of bad things.

_____

_____

_____

_____

_____

_____

_____

_____

_____

_____

_____

_____

_____

_____

_____

Intimacy
PARTNER 2 NEEDS

Identify the level of the intimacy you currently receive from your partner by shading up to the wave level. It's crucial to be open and sincere. Your partner won't be able to adapt to your needs unless they understand what's missing.

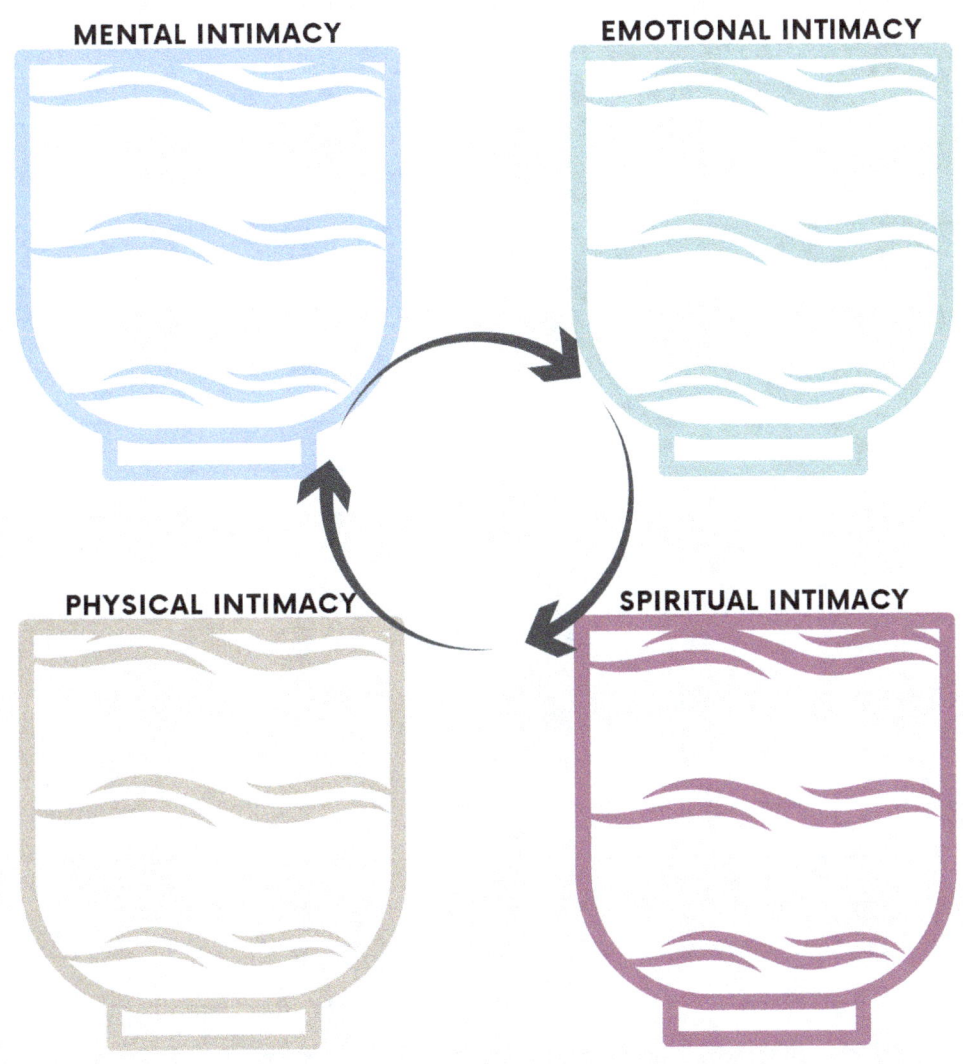

MENTAL INTIMACY

EMOTIONAL INTIMACY

PHYSICAL INTIMACY

SPIRITUAL INTIMACY

COMMUNICATING TOGETHER

Congratulations on successfully completing a challenging journey. Throughout this experience, you have mastered the SMART method for setting goals collaboratively. You've delved into self and relationship accountability, pushing beyond your comfort zones. Together, you have enhanced trust by learning how to articulate thoughts and communicate effectively during tough discussions. Additionally, you've recognized various forms of relationship intimacy. Utilize these tools to engage in open communication and how it affects 'The Relationship'. Work together to understand the impact of specific topics on your relationship and plan a path forward.

PARTNER 1

_____
_____
_____
_____
_____
_____
_____
_____
_____
_____

PARTNER 2

_____
_____
_____
_____
_____
_____
_____
_____
_____
_____

THE RELATIONSHIP

_____
_____
_____
_____
_____
_____
_____
_____

Intimacy
RELATIONSHIP NEEDS

Identify the level of intimacy you and your partner feel The Relationship currently receives from both of you by shading up to the wave level. It's crucial to be open and sincere. Imagine your relationship as a living entity, constantly evolving and growing. By acknowledging the level of intimacy you and your partner are providing, you can nurture and strengthen this bond. Remember, the relationship exists independently of each of you, with its own set of needs. By coming together and understanding these dynamics, you can navigate the levels of intimacy with grace and compassion.

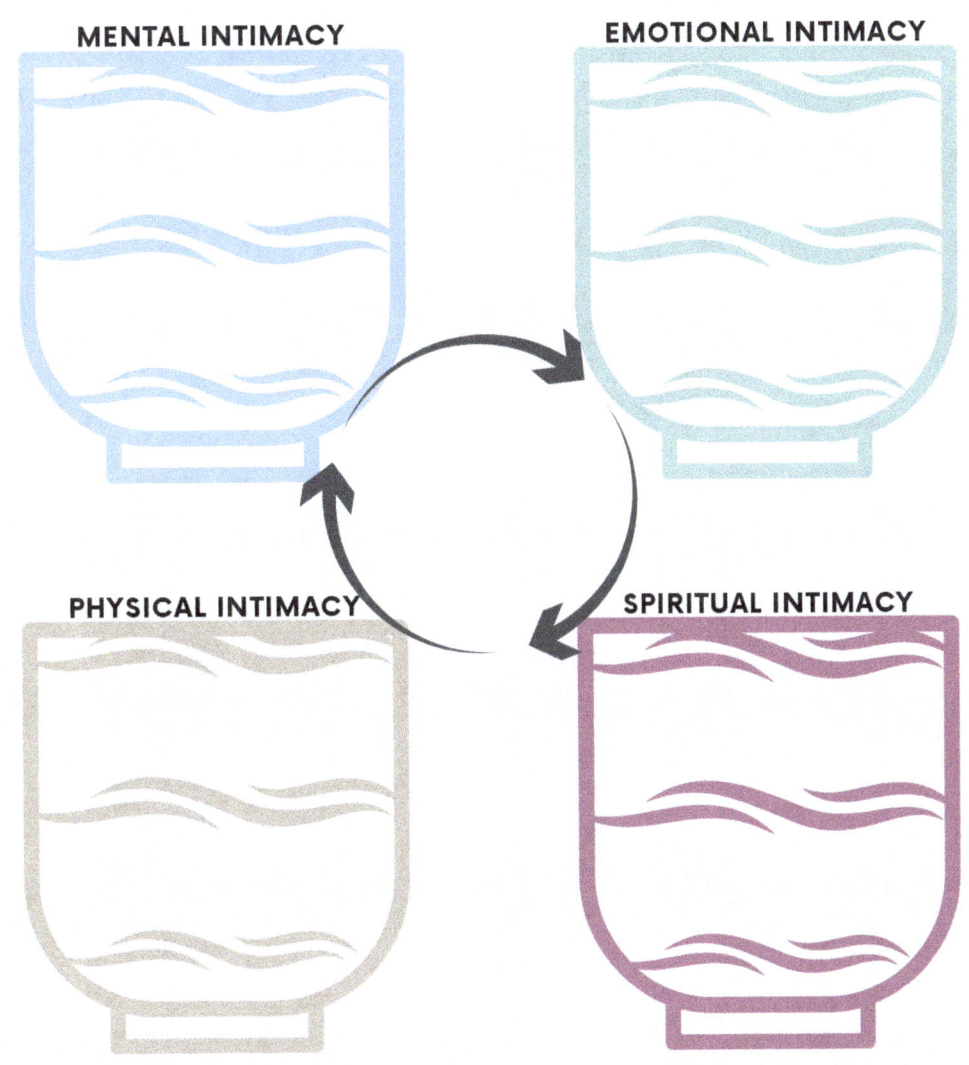

MENTAL INTIMACY

EMOTIONAL INTIMACY

PHYSICAL INTIMACY

SPIRITUAL INTIMACY

Week

FOUR

YOUR TURN

Your beginning doesn't have to dictate where The Relationship ends up. By developing your mind, heart, and spirit, you can guide the relationship back to a healthy, stable path and enhance its bond to help it thrive.

No peeking at Partner 2's section unless you both have decided to exchange sections before your planned meeting.

Weekly Plan

PARTNER 1

DATE:

M T W T F S S

3 THINGS I AM GRATEFUL FOR:

1.
2.
3.

ISSUES:

SOLUTION:

INTIMACY LEVEL:

ACCOUNTABILITY LEVEL:

5 PRIORITIES:
- ○
- ○
- ○
- ○
- ○

THINGS TO GET DONE:
- ○
- ○
- ○
- ○
- ○

DATE NIGHT IDEAS:
- ○
- ○
- ○
- ○
- ○

MOOD:

RELATIONSHIP GOALS:
1. ○
2. ○
3. ○
4. ○
5. ○

AFFIRMATIONS:

FINANCIAL GOALS:
1.
2.
3.

NOTES:

USE THE NOTES AREA TO ELABORATE ON ISSUES, SELF REFLECTION, AND HOLDING YOURSELF ACCOUNTABLE FOR YOUR CONTRIBUTION TO THE ISSUES. SHARE WITH EACH OTHER DAILY.

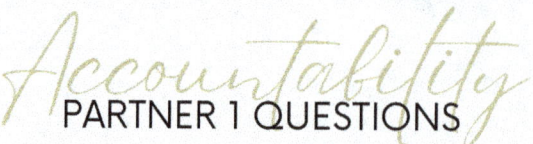

Accountability
PARTNER 1 QUESTIONS

Take this time to work through any issues from the week. Be honest with yourself so can reflect on how you contributed to the situations to prepare for your weekly discussion.

DID I PUT IN MY MAXIMUM EFFORT?

DID I ASK IF I NEEDED ANY HELP?

AM I COMPLETELY TRUTHFUL WITH MYSELF AND THOSE AROUND ME?

DID I AVOID DISTRACTIONS, TEMPTATION, AND PROCRASTINATION?

AM I SATISFIED WITH MY ACTIONS?

HOW CAN I DO BETTER NEXT TIME?

Message

PARTNER 1 "I" METHOD

By employing this approach, you eliminate the tendency to assign blame. Instead of saying "You did", "He did", or "But, She did", using "I" messages helps you communicate your feelings and requirements without shifting blame. Prioritize honesty with yourself first, as betraying yourself is the most severe form of betrayal, then extend that honesty to your partner as not being truthful is equally damaging as self-betrayal.

WHAT ARE MY TRUE FEELINGS?
START WITH "I FEEL/FELT ...."

WHAT WERE THE ACTIONS THAT OFFENDED ME?
START WITH "WHEN .... HAPPENS/HAPPENED"

ULTIMATELY THIS CAUSE ME TO?
START WITH "BECAUSE OF THIS I ...."

WHAT I NEED?
START WITH "I NEED ....
COMMUNICATION/ACTION TO BETTER UNDERSTAND".

Construct Your "I" Message

_____

_____

_____

_____

_____

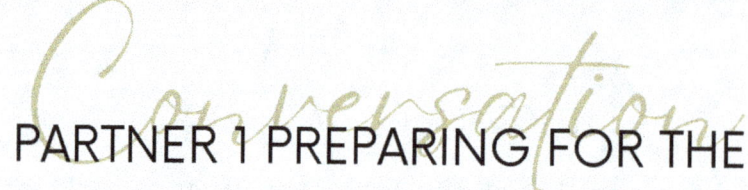

PARTNER 1 PREPARING FOR THE

Before engaging in a Difficult Conversation, take some time to work through the following worksheet for self-reflection on your thoughts. Schedule a specific time and day to address Difficult Conversations with your partner. If you need to reschedule, that's fine - but don't avoid or delay it. It's crucial not to ambush or bombard your partner. When you are both in a stable emotional and mental state, you are open for discussion and resolution of concerns.

What is the purpose behind the conversation?

What do you hope to accomplish?

Are your emotions altering your perception?

Did you satisfy all the Assertive Communication checks?

Did you complete your Self-Accountability assessment?

What outcome would you like?

PARTNER 1

Remember, lack of communication and bad communication both lead to the ending of a good thing; good communication leads to the end of bad things.

_____

_____

_____

_____

_____

_____

_____

_____

_____

_____

_____

_____

_____

_____

_____

_____

Intimacy
PARTNER 1 NEEDS

Identify the level of the intimacy you currently receive from your partner by shading up to the wave level. It's crucial to be open and sincere. Your partner won't be able to adapt to your needs unless they understand what's missing.

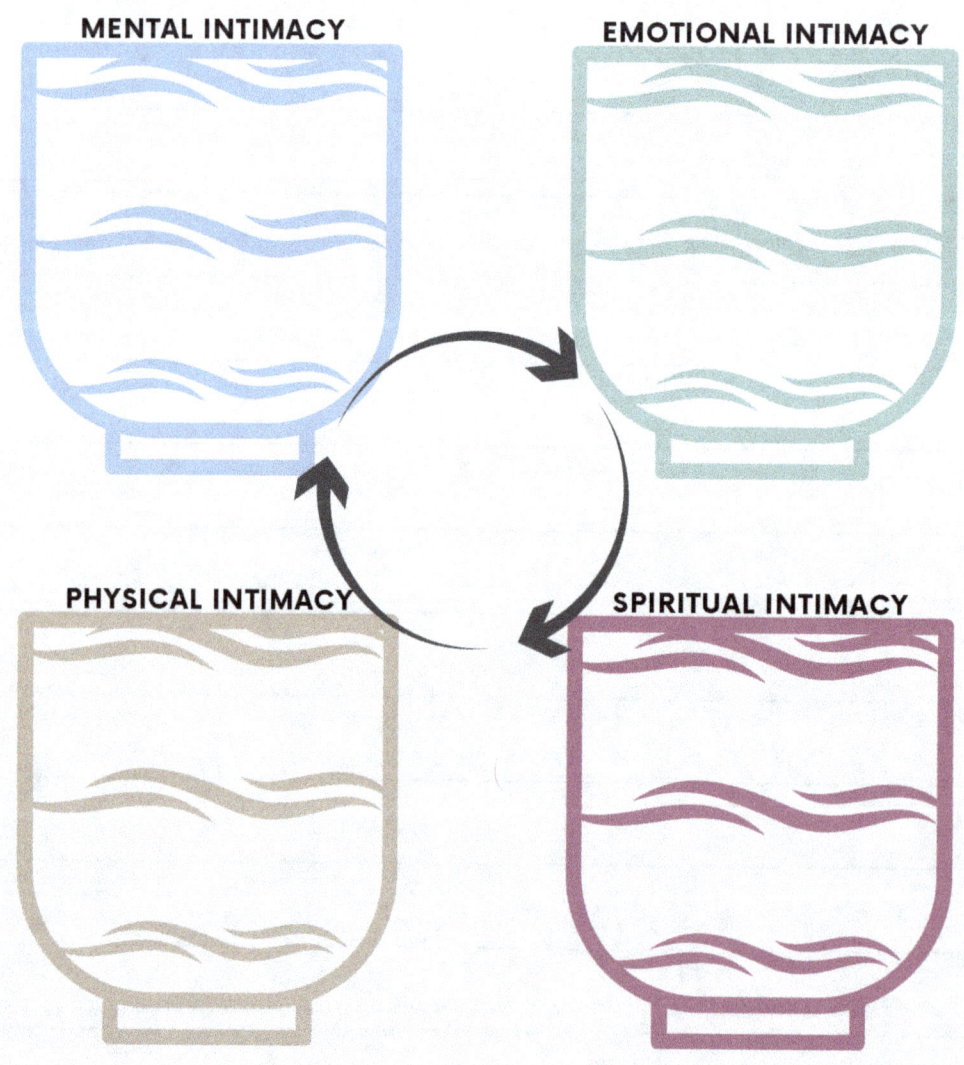

MENTAL INTIMACY

EMOTIONAL INTIMACY

PHYSICAL INTIMACY

SPIRITUAL INTIMACY

Partner 2

YOUR TURN

No peeking at Partner 1's section unless you both
have decided to exchange sections before your
planned meeting.

Weekly Plan

PARTNER 2

DATE:

M T W T F S S

3 THINGS I AM GRATEFUL FOR:

1. _____
2. _____
3. _____

ISSUES:

SOLUTION:

INTIMACY LEVEL:

ACCOUNTABILITY LEVEL:

5 PRIORITIES:

○ _____
○ _____
○ _____
○ _____
○ _____

THINGS TO GET DONE:

○ _____
○ _____
○ _____
○ _____
○ _____

DATE NIGHT IDEAS:

○ _____
○ _____
○ _____
○ _____
○ _____

MOOD:

RELATIONSHIP GOALS:

1. _____ ○
2. _____ ○
3. _____ ○
4. _____ ○
5. _____ ○

AFFIRMATIONS:

FINANCIAL GOALS:

1. _____
2. _____
3. _____

NOTES:

USE THE NOTES AREA TO ELABORATE ON ISSUES, SELF REFLECTION, AND HOLDING YOURSELF ACCOUNTABLE FOR YOUR CONTRIBUTION TO THE ISSUES. SHARE WITH EACH OTHER DAILY.

Take this time to work through any issues from the week. Be honest with yourself so can reflect on how you contributed to the situations to prepare for your weekly discussion.

DID I PUT IN MY MAXIMUM EFFORT?

DID I ASK IF I NEEDED ANY HELP?

AM I COMPLETELY TRUTHFUL WITH MYSELF AND THOSE AROUND ME?

DID I AVOID DISTRACTIONS, TEMPTATION, AND PROCRASTINATION?

AM I SATISFIED WITH MY ACTIONS?

HOW CAN I DO BETTER NEXT TIME?

By employing this approach, you eliminate the tendency to assign blame. Instead of saying "You did", "He did", or "But, she did", using "I" messages helps you communicate your feelings and requirements without shifting blame. Prioritize honesty with yourself first, as betraying yourself is the most severe form of betrayal, then extend that honesty to your partner as not being truthful is equally damaging as self-betrayal.

WHAT ARE MY TRUE FEELINGS?
START WITH "I FEEL/FELT ...."

WHAT WERE THE ACTIONS THAT OFFENDED ME?
START WITH "WHEN .... HAPPENS/HAPPENED"

ULTIMATELY THIS CAUSE ME TO?
START WITH "BECAUSE OF THIS I ...."

WHAT I NEED?
START WITH "I NEED .... COMMUNICATION/ACTION TO BETTER UNDERSTAND".

Construct Your "I" Message

_____

_____

_____

_____

_____

PARTNER 2 PREPARING FOR THE
Conversation

Before engaging in a Difficult Conversation, take some time to work through the following worksheet for self-reflection on your thoughts. Schedule a specific time and day to address Difficult Conversations with your partner. If you need to reschedule, that's fine - but don't avoid or delay it. It's crucial not to ambush or bombard your partner. When you are both in a stable emotional and mental state, you are open for discussion and resolution of concerns.

What is the purpose behind the conversation?

What do you hope to accomplish?

Are your emotions altering your perception?

Did you satisfy all the Assertive Communication checks?

Did you complete your Self-Accountability assessment?

What outcome would you like?

Communication
PARTNER 2

Remember, lack of communication and bad communication both lead to the ending of a good thing; good communication leads to the end of bad things.

_____
_____
_____
_____
_____
_____
_____
_____
_____
_____
_____
_____
_____
_____
_____

Intimacy
PARTNER 2 NEEDS

Identify the level of intimacy you currently receive from your partner by shading up to the wave level. It's crucial to be open and sincere. Your partner won't be able to adapt to your needs unless they understand what's missing.

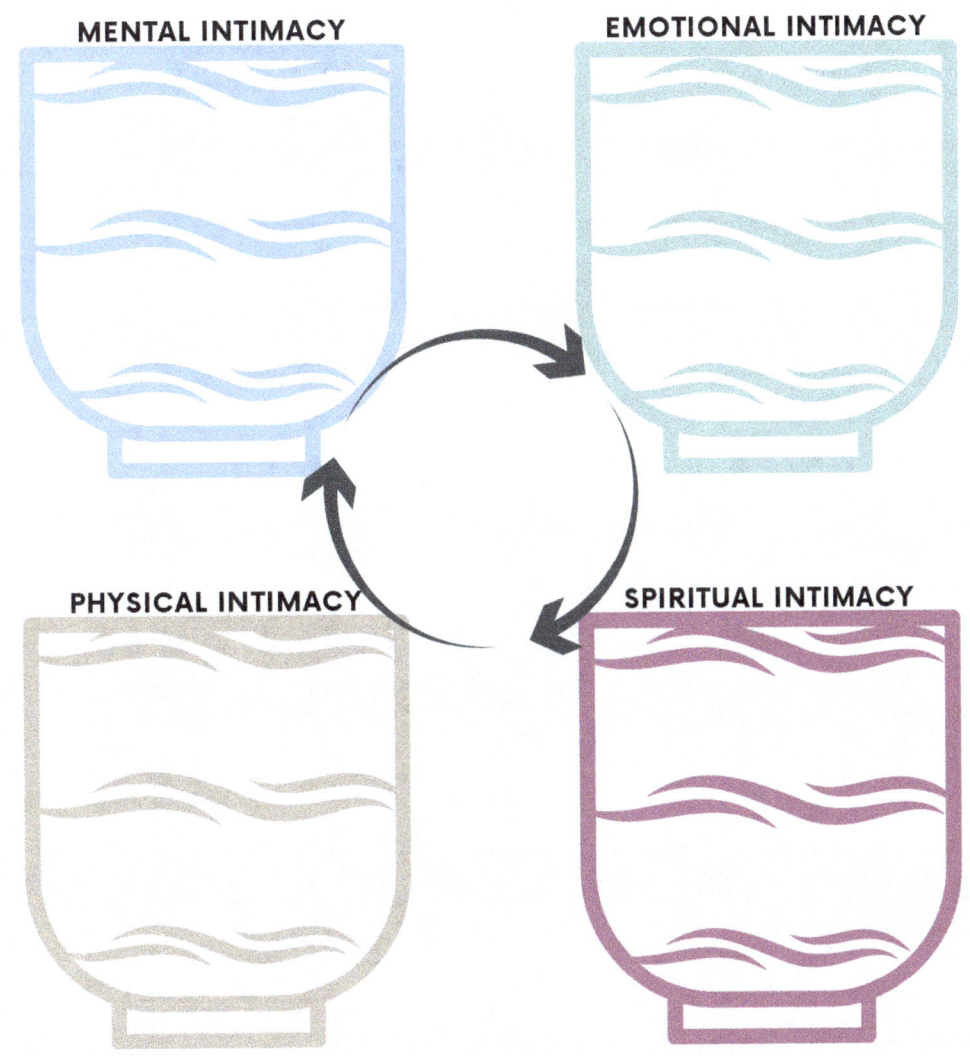

MENTAL INTIMACY

EMOTIONAL INTIMACY

PHYSICAL INTIMACY

SPIRITUAL INTIMACY

COMMUNICATING TOGETHER

Congratulations on successfully completing a challenging journey. Throughout this experience, you have mastered the SMART method for setting goals collaboratively. You've delved into self and relationship accountability, pushing beyond your comfort zones. Together, you have enhanced trust by learning how to articulate thoughts and communicate effectively during tough discussions. Additionally, you've recognized various forms of relationship intimacy. Utilize these tools to engage in open communication and how it affects 'The Relationship'. Work together to understand the impact of specific topics on your relationship and plan a path forward.

PARTNER 1

_____
_____
_____
_____
_____
_____
_____
_____
_____
_____

PARTNER 2

_____
_____
_____
_____
_____
_____
_____
_____
_____
_____

THE RELATIONSHIP

_____
_____
_____
_____
_____
_____
_____

Intimacy
RELATIONSHIP NEEDS

Identify the level of the intimacy you and your partner feel The Relationship currently receives from both of you by shading up to the wave level. It's crucial to be open and sincere. Imagine your relationship as a living entity, constantly evolving and growing. By acknowledging the level of intimacy you and your partner are providing, you can nurture and strengthen this bond. Remember, the relationship exists independently of each of you, with its own set of needs. By coming together and understanding these dynamics, you can navigate the levels of intimacy with grace and compassion.

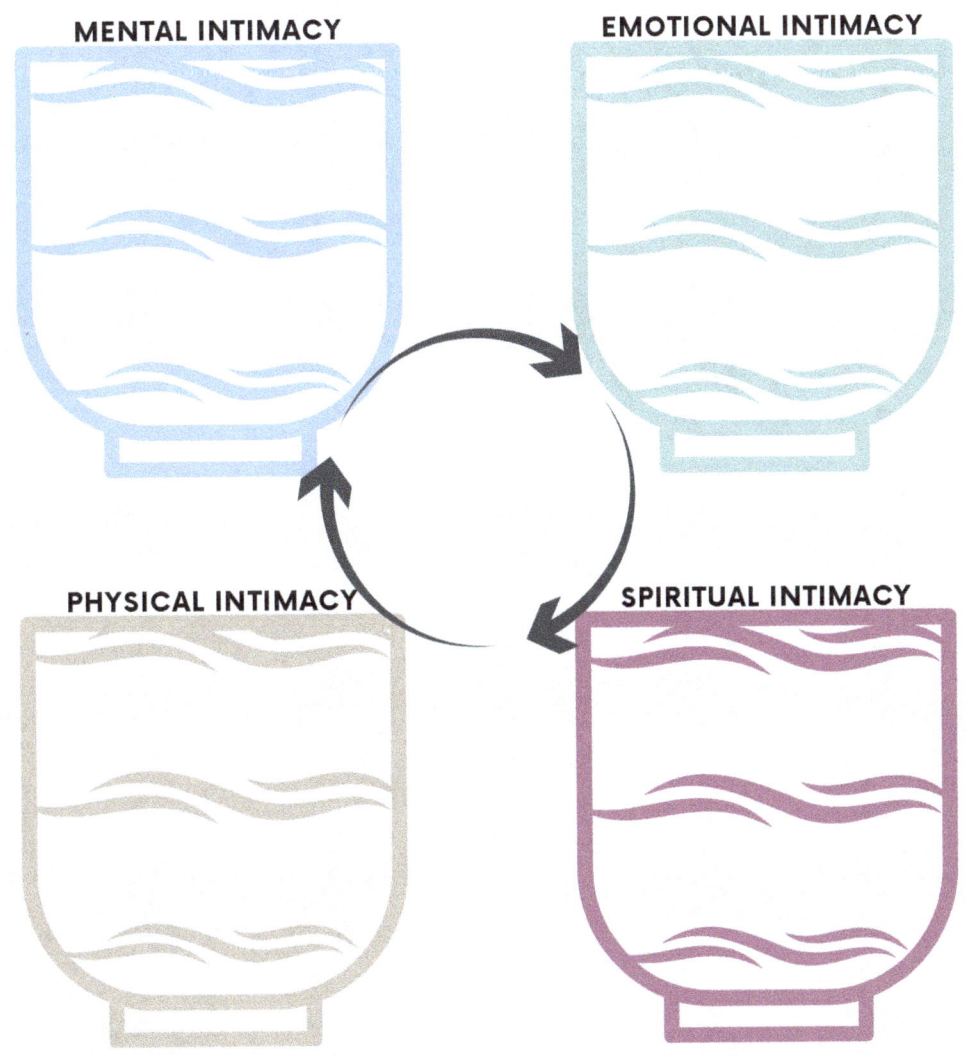

MENTAL INTIMACY

EMOTIONAL INTIMACY

PHYSICAL INTIMACY

SPIRITUAL INTIMACY

Reflect

AND ADJUST

While reflecting and adjusting, look at the bigger picture. Aim to nurture your personal growth and your Partner's growth every day. Prioritize The Relationship and recognize it as a distinct entity with specific needs. The development of the bond benefits not only you but also your loved ones and anyone who witnesses the unique connection between both of you.

Final Plan

TOGETHER

DATE:

M T W T F S S

3 THINGS WE ARE GRATEFUL FOR:

1. _____
2. _____
3. _____

ISSUES:

SOLUTION:

INTIMACY LEVEL:

ACCOUNTABILITY LEVEL:

5 PRIORITIES:
○ _____
○ _____
○ _____
○ _____
○ _____

THINGS TO GET DONE:
○ _____
○ _____
○ _____
○ _____
○ _____

DATE NIGHT IDEAS:
○ _____
○ _____
○ _____
○ _____
○ _____

MOOD:

RELATIONSHIP GOALS:
1. ○
2. ○
3. ○
4. ○
5. ○

AFFIRMATIONS:

FINANCIAL GOALS:
1.
2.
3.

FOR THE NEXT TWO DAYS, TAKE THE TIME TO READ THROUGH THIS GUIDE FROM START TO FINISH. REFLECT ON YOUR REACTIONS AND RESPONSES TO VARIOUS SITUATIONS OVER THE PAST MONTH. MODIFY YOUR GOALS IF NECESSARY OR SET NEW ONES. BE KIND TO EACH OTHER. REMEMBER, IT TAKES 30 DAYS TO FORM A HABIT AND 90 DAYS TO ESTABLISH A NEW LIFESTYLE. AIM FOR ANOTHER 60 DAYS AND EMBRACE GENUINE EVOLUTION.

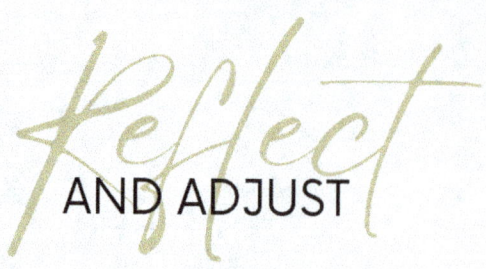

Reflect
AND ADJUST

What things can WE improve or focus on next month?

_____

_____

_____

_____

_____

_____

What moments of personal growth did WE experience?

_____

_____

_____

_____

_____

_____

_____

Reflect
AND ADJUST

What challenges did WE overcome and how did WE overcome them?

_____

_____

_____

_____

_____

_____

Who are the significant people in our lives and why?

_____

_____

_____

_____

_____

_____

Reflect
AND ADJUST

What ways did WE give back or make a positive impact
to The Relationship?

_____

_____

_____

_____

_____

_____

What are the Positive habits WE developed and want
to maintain?

_____

_____

_____

_____

_____

_____

_____

AND ADJUST

What did WE learned about our relationship?

_____

_____

_____

_____

_____

_____

_____

What limiting beliefs were we embracing that WE have discovered?

_____

_____

_____

_____

_____

_____

_____

Reflect
AND ADJUST

Were any limiting beliefs true or have WE been using them as an excuse?

_____

_____

_____

_____

_____

_____

_____

How have these beliefs been harmful to us individually
and The Relationship?

_____

_____

_____

_____

_____

_____

_____

AND ADJUST

Moving forward, what do WE plan to do?

_____

_____

_____

_____

_____

_____

_____

_____

_____

_____

_____

_____

_____

Evolve

TO BE CONTINUED...

Finding a therapist within the African American community can present significant challenges. Below are some resources to assist you in your search.

African American Therapists

African American Marriage Counseling

Regain

AFAM Oasis

Explore More

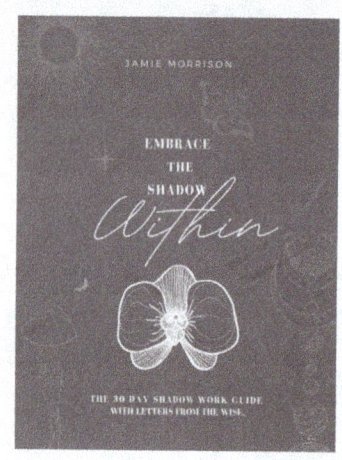

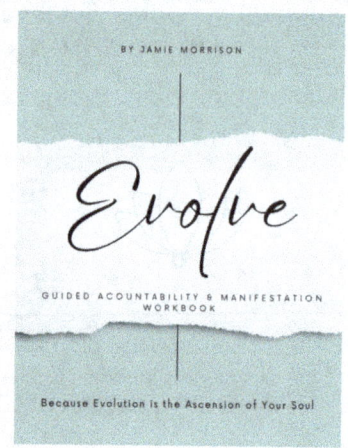